T0303108

My learn
cook book
Kitchen
CONTENTS
Chocolate Cake
Icing (Chocolate)
PRESERVES JAMS
PICKLES SAUCES
SUNDRIES

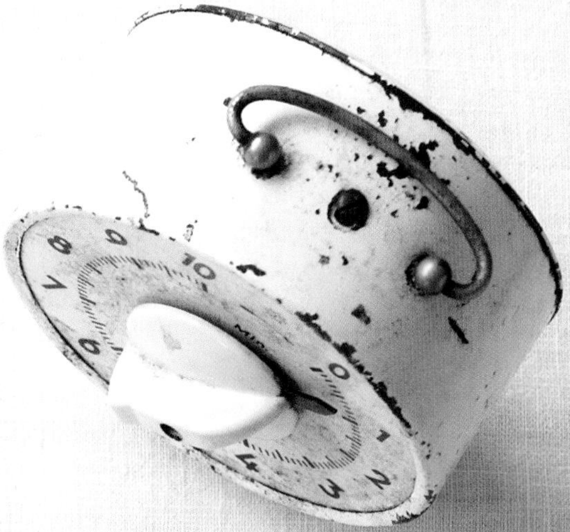

# MY FAVOURITE FOOD for All Seasons

JANELLE BLOOM

PHOTOGRAPHY BY STEVE BROWN

EBURY PRESS

# CONTENTS

PEANUT BUTTER BROWNIES
PAGE 176

# INTRODUCTION

The name of this, my latest cookbook, ***My Favourite Food for All Seasons***, conveys a clear picture of the beautiful and, yes, delicious pages that follow. Sharing my food, recipes and tips has always been my number one passion, yet having this opportunity also to impart my knowledge and love of fresh seasonal produce is very gratifying. Blessed by the wonderful part of the world we live in, the vast land and diverse climate, we are spoilt by the quality of stunning food we have within our reach all year round, my main reason for writing this book.

During my research, I asked many people to give me the word or phrase they associate with summer, autumn, winter and spring. The responses were overwhelmingly similar. Summer: 'hot' or 'beach'. Spring: 'picnic', 'lighter clothes' and 'diet time'. Autumn: 'falling leaves'. Winter: 'football' or 'sleep-ins'. For me, summer is a mango. Spring: asparagus. Autumn: baking and roasts. Winter: avocado and crumbles. I know it's no surprise that I think about food, but I was surprised that, as our weather changes, many of us don't shift the way we think about the food we cook. In winter we might occasionally add a soup or casserole. In summer we might replace vegies with salad on the plate, but we mainly cook the same repertoire of recipes over and over. I hope this book will inspire much more variety as the seasons change.

While working on this book, on and off for about ten years, I have seen many changes, the biggest being the power of supermarkets and their impact on the way we shop. A vast range of fruit and vegetables is now available all year round, with new varieties popping up all the time, so our knowledge of what's in season has been lost. We all know the fresh cherries in store in June and July come from the US, but how often do we pick up oranges in late summer without realising they are from Israel or that the fresh peas and garlic come from China? It's a minefield and an issue I am very passionate about. Knowledge is power, so knowing what's in season locally and at its peak for flavour and nutrition (and good for our hip pocket) is a huge part of the way I cook. I have always been an advocate of shopping at the local greengrocer, butcher and farmers' markets – this is where we learn about the best buys of the day.

As you turn the pages of this book, my fourth in as many years, I hope it will take you on a journey through the changing seasons – and fill you with inspirational ideas to cook for yourself, your family and your friends. My focus hasn't changed; my food has always been centred on feeding the ones we love delicious home-cooked food that's easy to re-create with minimal fuss and minimal preservatives. ***My Favourite Food*** is no exception.

The book is split into seasonal chapters for sweet and savoury, but feel no guilt about cooking slow-cooked shoulder of lamb in summer or serving roasted tomatoes and bocconcini salad in winter – the majority of recipes can be served all year round. The month-by-month 'Best Buys' sections are there to empower you with knowledge of the best seasonal produce and, for some, their varieties. The 'Produce' pages expand on this knowledge, as well as providing great hints and tips that I know you will find useful on a daily basis.

If you're like me and you love your family and friends, love life, food and the freedom of choice, then enjoy, inspire and create the food from ***My Favourite Food for All Seasons*** with joy in your heart and a smile on your face. There is no greater joy than conversing around a table laden with home-cooked food using fresh seasonal ingredients!

To your fun, food-filled days ahead,

*Janelle*

# Q&A WITH JANELLE

*What is your food philosophy?*
It's a pretty simple one: cook with as many fresh ingredients as you can, limiting the number of preservatives, additives and chemicals that come in packets, cans, bottles and pre-prepared foods. Enjoy all the yummy things in moderation, and get 5 serves of fresh vegetables and 2 serves of fresh fruit each and every day.

*Who has been your greatest culinary inspiration?*
I would have to say Maggie Beer. When I watch Maggie and read her recipes and comments, she really inspires me. Maggie is everything I hope to be (and soon, as age and time are catching me): a great cook; very generous in sharing her knowledge and skill; a kind, gentle soul who is well respected by both the public and within the industry.

*How did you get into TV?*
It was a chance meeting with Gabriel Gaté who introduced me to his TV producer at the time, Rhonda Byrne (yes, the lady who wrote *The Secret*). I had no idea why at the time since I never wanted to be on TV – I wanted to be a magazine food editor. One appearance on *What's Cooking,* the rest is history. It gave me the opportunity to break through some personal barriers, which has been good for me. Though it's important to say I have worked hard and there have been many highs and lows, as in everyone's careers, but I have always just tried to give 100 per cent, stay true to who I am and remember it's only a job – a balanced life is so important.

*As a successful cookbook author you must feel a huge sense of achievement. What is the formula to a bestseller?*
I think any author who gets a book on the shelf in this competitive market has a level of success. Sales is another form of success. The sense of pride and achievement is huge. Everyone in their day-to-day life has doubts about their self-worth and confidence, me included. Having four tangible books to pick up, ones that people have purchased, is a good boost to my confidence and sense of achievement. The formula for a bestseller is in the hands of the public, book stores and the publisher's distribution – as an author, all you can do is be true to yourself and your readers.

*You have worked in television, magazines, radio. Do you have a secret love for one?*
They are all different. I enjoy television (who would have thought!) because the jobs I have had are loads of fun and the people I have met are friends for life – the behind-the-scenes crew are some of the best people you could ever hope to meet. Radio is live and on the spot, and I thrive on this. Magazines can be great too, but there are so many restrictions – it's the hardest medium of them all.

*As an original* Ready Steady Cook *chef, it looks like you all have a lot of fun on the show. Is there much friendly competition as well?*
It's very competitive in a friendly way. It's all about winning between the chefs, but I also like to make sure my contestant has a great time and people at home are inspired by what I cook. I love beating Alistair and Manu (although Manu has left the show now).

*You have been a volunteer at Ronald McDonald House for 5 years now. What is the most rewarding part of your volunteer work?*
The kids and families have touched my life like no one else has. I got involved after spending time at the hospital with my sister, who was very sick. There were so many people who helped her that I decided when she was on the road to recovery I would give back. Working in a place like Ronald McDonald House brings a sense of humility to your life. It makes you realise many people are doing it tough. The spunk and spirit the kids and their families possess is inspirational. I truly value the time I get to spend in the house with amazing people, including staff and other volunteers. I encourage everyone to do a little volunteer work – you won't regret it.

*What would you list as your favourite cookbooks?*
All of Jamie Oliver's books – I often cook from them. Marcella Hazan's *The Classic Italian Cook Book*. *Baking with Julia* (Julia Child, of course). *Everyday Italian* by Giada De Laurentiis.

*What is one thing we may not know about you?*
I am shy and a pretty private person. My dear friend Pete Everett has extracted a lot of personal information about me over the years on RSC, which I know is a good thing for viewers, but I sometimes forget I am not sitting on the couch having a drink with Pete. I am on national TV!

*Favourite savoury food:*
Barbecue lamb cutlets and double-fried home-made chips with loads of salad, of course.

*Favourite sweet food:*
A great apple crumble.

*Favourite ingredient:*
Good-quality olive oil – it can lift an average dish.

*Favourite kitchen appliance:*
I have a few, but my new Electrolux oven cooks to perfection. (No, I am not paid to say this. Yes, I did buy it.)

*One thing you love about your kitchen:*
It's big, bright with loads of natural light and plenty of bench space.

*How would you like to be remembered?*
I try not to worry about what other people think – what's important to me is my family and friends who love and trust me.

# SUMMER

*Blue skies, sandy feet, ice-cold cocktails on the deck with friends and the sweet aroma of summer's fruit as you walk into the greengrocer. These are the things I love about summer.*

# BEST BUYS

## FRUIT

### DECEMBER

*apricots*
*berries:*
  *raspberries, blueberries, blackberries, strawberries and red currants*
*cherries*
*lychees*
*mangoes:*
  *Kensington Pride, R2E2, Calypso, Honey Gold*
*oranges:*
  *Valencia*
*peaches:*
  *yellow clingstone*
*pineapples*
*rhubarb*
*watermelon*

### JANUARY

*apricots*
*berries:*
  *blackberries, strawberries and blueberries*
*cherries*
*limes*
*mangoes:*
  *Kensington Pride, Calypso, R2E2, Honey Gold, Kiett*
*nectarines:*
  *yellow and white freestone*
*passionfruit*
*peaches:*
  *yellow and white freestone*
*plums:*
  *blood and amber*

### FEBRUARY

*bananas*
*figs*
*grapes:*
  *Menindee, Red Globe, Flame*
*limes*
*lychees*
*mangoes:*
  *Kensington Pride, Calypso, R2E2, Honey Gold, Kiett, Kent, Pearl*
*nectarines:*
  *yellow and white freestone*
*passionfruit*
*peaches:*
  *yellow and white freestone*
*pineapples*
*plums:*
  *Angelina, sugar plum*
*strawberries*
*watermelon and rockmelon*

# VEGETABLES

## DECEMBER

*Asian greens*
*asparagus*
*avocados:*
  *Hass, Reed*
*beans:*
  *green and butter*
*capsicum:*
  *red, yellow and green*
*celery*
*cucumber:*
  *Lebanese and telegraph*
*eggplant*
*lettuce:*
  *baby, cos and iceberg*
*radishes*
*sweet corn and baby corn*
*tomatoes*

## JANUARY

*Asian greens:*
  *on choy*
*avocados:*
  *Hass, Reed, Shepard*
*beans:*
  *green, snake, flat and butter*
*capsicum:*
  *red, yellow and green*
*celery*
*chillies*
*eggplant*
*garlic*
*lettuce:*
  *cos and iceberg*
*onions:*
  *red, brown, white and green*
*peas:*
  *green, sugar and snap*
*snowpeas*
*zucchini*
*zucchini flowers*

## FEBRUARY

*avocados:*
  *Shepard*
*beans:*
  *green and snake*
*Chinese cabbage*
*lettuce*
*pumpkin:*
  *butternut*
*radishes*
*sweet corn*
*tomatoes*
*zucchini*

# PRODUCE

## PEACHES & NECTARINES

Early season fruit is yellow and clingstone – as the name suggests, the stone clings to the fruit, so these are best eaten fresh or poached whole. Freestone fruit arrives mid season. It's easy to eat, peel and cook. White peaches and nectarines are spectacular. When ripe, they are sweeter and juicier, and have a more intense flavour than the yellow varieties.

*Storage:* Ripe but firm stone fruit will soften at room temperature for 1–2 days. Always remove them from plastic bags. Store ripe fruit on a plate in the fridge crisper for 2–3 days.

*Tip*: Wash in a bowl of cold water just before you eat (not under running water as this can bruise the fruit).

*Best buddies with:* Vanilla, cinnamon, ginger, honey, maple syrup and brown sugar, lemons and limes, berries, almonds, pistachio and macadamia nuts, sparkling wine and dairy.

## PLUMS

Santa Rosa, Amber, Angelina and Mariposa (also called blood plum) are the pick to bite into. When cooking, Angelina, Mariposa and President are my preferences.

*Storage:* Plums are the most perishable of all stone fruit, so treat with TLC. Allow firm fruit to ripen in a single layer at room temperature until the fruit yields under gentle pressure. Once ripe, store in the vegetable crisper for 3–4 days.

*Tip:* Don't stack fruit in the fruit bowl or fridge – it will cause the fruit to bruise and the skin to split.

*Cooking:* Plums make the very best crumbles. They are great roasted or stewed over ice-cream or baked in tarts, cakes and muffins. They are difficult to peel, so cook with skin on. With their high natural pectin (found in the seed), they are perfect for jams, chutneys and sauces. Remove the seeds and wrap them in muslin, and drop into the pan while cooking jam.

*Best buddies with:* Soft cheese like ricotta, brie and goats' curd, apples and oranges, vanilla, cinnamon, nutmeg and cloves, almonds and walnuts.

## MANGOES

One of summer's treats is biting into a chilled, sweet, juicy mango and letting the sticky juice run down your arm. Familiarise yourself with the varieties as they are quite different.

Kensington Pride or Bowen are the first mangoes to hit the greengrocer, usually in late October. They are sweet, juicy, very fragrant and my favourite.

Calypso have a stunning bright orange-pink blush skin. They are fibreless, have a small seed and firmer in texture and are not as sweet as KP. If the weather's good, they have a long season.

Honey Gold taste even better than they look. They have a yellow-pink skin, sweet aroma, firm juicy sweet, fibreless flesh and a very good shelf life.

R2E2 has a stunning crimson blush on the skin. Its firmer, less juicy flesh makes it great for cooking.

Thai or green mangoes are a variety, not early-picked fruit. Best used in Asian cooking to make salsas, salads and chutneys.

*Storage:* Allow firm fruit to ripen in the fruit bowl out of direct sunlight. Once ripe, store loose in the fridge crisper for up to 5 days.

*Best buddies with:* Lemons and limes, vanilla, macadamia nuts, vanilla ice-cream and cream, brown sugar, coconut, ginger, salad leaves, prawns and chicken.

## AVOCADOS

Available all year – as the seasons change, so does the variety. It's one of the ingredients I could not live without.

Hass is my favourite; its pebbly-textured skin makes it easy to identify. It is the only variety to change skin colour as it ripens. Unripe it is green, but gradually turns purple-black.

Fuerte is a pear-shaped avocado with a thin, smooth, dull-green skin. They are easy to peel and have a rich, smooth, buttery texture.

Sharwill are similar to fuerte in flavour, however their skin is a little pebbly and they are rounder in shape.

Reed are large, almost round in shape, with a slightly textured deep-green skin. They have a smooth, buttery texture and are better chopped or diced. They are watery when mashed.

Shepard have a smooth green skin, which does not turn black as they ripen. They are the only variety that does not go brown when cut.

*Tip:* To speed up ripening, place them into a brown paper bag with a ripe banana and seal it. Store in fruit bowl. The banana gives off ethylene gas, which speeds up the ripening process.

*Storage:* Unripe avocados should be stored in a single layer (to prevent bruising) in a dry, airy place. To slow the ripening process, place them in the fridge crisper. Once ripe, an avocado will keep 2–3 days in the fridge.

*Best buddies with:* Olive oil, bacon, chicken and turkey, white fish and shell fish, chilli, all citrus, tomatoes, cucumber, green onions, mild cheese, crisp lettuce, mint, parsley and coriander – the pick of the herbs.

## TOMATOES

Botanically a tropical fruit related to eggplants and capsicums, we put them in the vegetable basket as they are mainly used in savoury dishes.

As a general rule, the Roma or plum tomato is best for cooking and drying, whether it be by the sun or in the oven. The old favourite ox-heart is making a comeback. It has minimal seeds so is great on sandwiches and bruschetta. Green tomatoes should be cooked – they make the best chutney – and all-purpose and cherry tomatoes are great raw in salads, marinated or roasted.

*Tip:* For the best flavour, eat them at room temperature. Truss tomatoes keep ripening in the fruit bowl, drawing nutrients from the stem.

*Storage:* Purchase in small quantities and store at room temperature. Refrigerating tomatoes causes the flesh to become soft, making them more suitable for cooking than eating raw.

*Best buddies with*: Olive oil, garlic, ginger and chilli, mild white fish and shellfish, mustard, eggs, cream, soft and hard cheese, yoghurt, soft herbs like basil, parsley and oregano.

## CORN

A barbecue in Australia isn't complete without the butter dripping down your arm as you bite into a fresh corncob.

*Storage*: Store corn wrapped in its husk in a plastic bag in the fridge crisper; best eaten within 2 days. Peel and remove the silks just prior to cooking. If corn is not in its husk, wrap in a damp tea towel and store in the crisper.

*Tip*: To remove the kernels, trim both ends so it stands flat on a board. Starting halfway down the cob, slice the kernels off. Turn and repeat with other half of the cob. The corn doesn't have as far to fall, which means it will pile onto the board, not the floor.

*Best buddies* with: Butter and olive oil; cream and sour cream; chilli and garlic; cumin, coriander and sweet paprika; chicken, fish and prawns; bacon, salty feta and goats' cheese; avocado, cucumber, capsicum and tomatoes.

## GREEN BEANS

Green beans are also known as French beans. The majority of beans now available are the stringless variety.

Baby beans are green beans that have been harvested early; they are smaller, sweeter and more expensive than regular green beans.

Italian flat beans, as the name suggests, are flat with pale-green pods that are up to 20cm long and 2cm wide. The pod is picked at the crisp snapping stage while the seeds are immature and soft. Both the pod and seeds are eaten.

Butter beans, or wax beans, are a pale-yellow variety of the green bean. They are similar in shape and size, and delicious when young and fresh.

Snake beans are a climbing green bean that are longer, thinner and coarser than the regular green bean. They are great for stir-frying and Asian-inspired salads.

*Best buddies with:* Butter, cream and yoghurt; olive oil; bacon, ham and prawns; mint, parsley and chives; walnuts; chilli and garlic.

*Storage*: Store unwashed beans in a plastic bag in the crisper part of the fridge for three days.

# SUMMER SAVOURY

# ROASTED CAULIFLOWER DIP

*I am always looking for new flavour combinations in dips. I was in Melbourne recently and tasted a cauliflower dip at a great restaurant called Baba Levantine Trading Company. I tried for months to work out how they made it – enjoy the rewards!*

SERVES 8

*400g cauliflower, trimmed*
*2 unpeeled garlic cloves*
*100ml extra-virgin olive oil*
*1 teaspoon ground cumin*
*400g can chickpeas, drained, rinsed*
*2 tablespoons organic tahini*
*½ lemon, juiced*
*⅓ cup Greek-style yoghurt* ✿
*2 teaspoons drained capers*
*1 tablespoon pine nuts, toasted*
*extra-virgin olive oil and baby rocket leaves, to serve*
*toasted Turkish bread, to serve*

1 Preheat oven to 200°C fan-forced/220°C no fan. Thinly slice the cauliflower and place into a roasting pan. Add the garlic to the pan, then drizzle with 2 tablespoons of the oil, sprinkle with cumin and season with salt and freshly ground black pepper, then toss to coat the cauliflower.

2 Roast for 12 minutes, stirring the cauliflower after 6 minutes, until just tender. Cover with a clean tea towel and set aside in the pan to cool to room temperature.

3 Squeeze the soft, roasted garlic from the skin. Combine roasted garlic, cauliflower, chickpeas, tahini, lemon juice and the remaining 60ml of oil in a food processor. Process until smooth. Transfer mixture to a bowl, taste and season with salt and pepper. Stir in the yoghurt, press a piece of plastic wrap onto the surface of the dip and refrigerate until ready to serve.

4 To serve, spoon dip onto a plate, scatter over the capers and pine nuts. Drizzle with a little extra-virgin olive oil and top with rocket if desired. Serve with Turkish bread.

✿ If time permits, spoon Greek yoghurt into a sieve lined with muslin and place over a bowl. Cover and refrigerate 4–8 hours to allow excess liquid to drain off, leaving a beautiful, thick yoghurt.

# SUMMER ANTIPASTO

*Antipasto is expensive to buy, but easy to make. It's fabulous on a platter with dips or used on pizzas, sandwiches, wraps and burgers. Roughly chopped and thrown into Bolognese, it turns an ordinary dish gourmet! Antipasto will keep 2–3 weeks in the fridge.*

ENOUGH FOR 8 PEOPLE

*1 red capsicum*
*1 yellow capsicum*
*½ butternut pumpkin, cut into 1cm-thick wedges*
*1 eggplant, cut into 1cm-thick slices*
*olive oil, for greasing*
*300g baby bocconcini*
*200g feta, cut into cubes*
*1 cup mixed olives*
*150g semi-dried tomatoes*
*4 marinated artichoke hearts, quartered*
*6 fresh bay leaves*
*1 long red chilli, quartered*
*1 long green chilli, quartered*
*6 sprigs rosemary, washed and dried*
*3 teaspoons black peppercorns*
*toasted crusty bread, to serve*

MARINADE

*750ml olive oil*
*200ml red wine vinegar*
*1 teaspoon caster sugar*
*1 teaspoon sea salt flakes, crushed*

1 Cut the capsicum into quarters, remove the centre core and all the seeds. Preheat the grill on high. Place the capsicum skin side up onto a baking tray. Grill for 6–8 minutes or until the skin turns black. Place capsicum into a snap lock bag and seal. Stand for 5 minutes. ♥ Use your fingers to peel and remove the skin. Cut into strips and set aside to cool completely.

2 Preheat a barbecue plate or grill over medium-high heat until hot. Place the pumpkin onto a microwave-safe plate in a single layer, cover and microwave for 3–4 minutes on High/100% until almost tender. Brush both sides of the eggplant and hot pumpkin with a little olive oil. Barbecue the vegetables for 3–4 minutes each side or until lightly charred and tender. Set aside to cool completely.

3 Pack the vegetables, cheese, olives, tomatoes, artichokes, bay leaves, chillies, rosemary and peppercorns alternately into jars until three-quarters full. (I used two, 2-litre sterilised glass jars.)

4 For the marinade, whisk all the dressing ingredients together then gradually pour into the jar, making sure there are no air pockets and all the ingredients are completely covered.

5 Refrigerate for at least 2–3 days to allow the flavours to develop. Serve with bread.

♥ The steam helps to lift the skin, making it easy to peel without rinsing under water, which dilutes the flavour.

# SEARED SIRLOIN WITH FRESH GREEN SALSA

SERVES 4

*600g piece beef sirloin* ✿
*2 tablespoons extra-virgin olive oil*
*2 tablespoons thyme leaves*
*baby cress, to serve*

FRESH GREEN SALSA

*1 small lemon, juiced*
*¼ cup extra-virgin olive oil*
*½ teaspoon caster sugar*
*1 teaspoon Dijon mustard*
*⅓ cup flat-leaf parsley, finely chopped*
*1 long green chilli, seeded, finely chopped*
*4 green onions, finely chopped*
*2 tablespoons drained baby capers, chopped*
*1 garlic clove, finely chopped*

1 For the fresh green salsa, whisk the lemon juice, oil, sugar, mustard and salt and pepper together in a bowl. Combine the parsley, chilli, green onions, capers and garlic and stir into the lemon mixture. Set aside.

2 Slice the piece of sirloin into eight thin steaks. Place onto a board in a single layer and flatten with a meat mallet until wafer-thin. Drizzle with olive oil, then scatter over the thyme leaves, season with salt and pepper. Use your fingertips to rub the oil and seasoning into both sides of the steak.

3 Heat a large, heavy-based frying pan over high heat until very hot. Cook the steak in batches for 30 seconds on each side, then transfer to a platter. Spoon the green salsa over the hot steaks, scatter over baby cress and serve with roasted tomato and mozzarella salad (see recipe page 44).

✿ You can ask your butcher to do this. Essentially, you need 8 thin 'minute' steaks flattened with a meat mallet.

# CHICKEN & DOUBLE-BACON CLUB SANDWICH

*Who doesn't love a club sandwich? Double bacon is a must, combined with mayo and home-made mango chutney – perfect for a summer lunch or dinner fare.*

SERVES 2

*2 teaspoons sumac spice* ♥
*1 (about 200g) single chicken breast fillet*
*1 tablespoon olive oil*
*4 slices bacon, rind removed, halved crossways*
*2 tablespoons quality whole egg mayonnaise*
*6 slices sourdough bread, toasted*
*½ ripe avocado, thinly sliced*
*handful mixed salad leaves*
*1 vine-ripened tomato, thinly sliced*

JANELLE'S MANGO CHUTNEY
MAKES 4 CUPS

*4 mangoes, peeled, chopped* *(see page 14)*
*2 Golden Delicious or Granny Smith apples, peeled, cored, chopped*
*2 cups brown sugar*
*100ml malt vinegar*
*1 tablespoon freshly grated ginger*
*1 small red chilli, seeds in, finely chopped*
*¼ teaspoon sea salt flakes, crushed*
*6 green onions, finely chopped*

1 For the mango chutney, combine the mango and apple in a large heat-proof microwave-safe bowl. Cover loosely with plastic wrap and microwave for 6 minutes on High/100% until the fruit is warm. Remove the plastic wrap and stir in the remaining ingredients. Microwave, uncovered, for a further 20–25 minutes on High/100%, stirring every 5 minutes or until chutney has thickened. Spoon the hot chutney into hot sterilised jars, seal. Turn upside down and stand 2 minutes, then turn right side up and allow to cool. Store in the fridge for up to 3 months.

2 Sprinkle the sumac evenly over both sides of the chicken. Heat the oil in a small non-stick frying pan over medium heat. Add the chicken and cook for 3–4 minutes each side or until cooked through. Transfer to a plate, cover and stand 5 minutes, then slice thinly across the grain.

3 Cook the bacon, in batches, in the same pan for 1–2 minutes each side or until crisp. Transfer to a plate lined with paper towel.

4 Spread the mayonnaise evenly over one side of each slice of toasted bread, then spread some mango chutney thickly over the mayonnaise.

5 Top two slices of the toast with half the bacon, then the avocado and half the salad leaves. Top with another slice of bread, mayonnaise side up. Top with chicken, remaining bacon, tomato and remaining lettuce. Sandwich together with the remaining toast, mayonnaise side down. Secure with a skewer, cut in half and serve.

♥ Sumac is a Middle Eastern spice that has a lemony sour taste. It's available in the spice section of the supermarket or online at www.herbies.com.au.

# SWEET & SPICY STICKY CHICKEN WINGS

*Chicken wings are both a family favourite and a budget dinner – I could eat them every night of the week. Served with a beautiful salad, dinner is on the table for a couple of dollars per person.*

SERVES 4

*2 tablespoons olive oil*
*2 stalks lemongrass, white and lime-green part only*
*1 lemon, rind finely grated*
*2 garlic cloves, chopped*
*2 eschalots, peeled, chopped* ✿
*2 tablespoons chilli jam (see recipe page 206)*
*2 tablespoons fish sauce*
*2 tablespoons brown sugar*
*16 chicken wings*

1 Combine the olive oil, lemongrass, lemon rind, garlic and eschalots in a small food processor. Process until finely chopped. Transfer to a bowl. Stir in the chilli jam, fish sauce and brown sugar.

2 Place chicken wings in a snap lock bag. Pour in the chilli jam mixture, secure and rub the marinade all over the chicken using your fingers. Refrigerate for 1 hour or overnight if time permits.

3 Preheat oven to 180°C fan-forced/200°C no fan. Lightly grease or line a large shallow roasting pan with baking paper. Remove the chicken from the marinade and arrange in a single layer in the roasting pan. Roast, basting occasionally with the marinade, for 30–35 minutes or until golden, sticky and cooked through. Serve with red salad (see recipe page 32).

✿ Eschalots are also known as French shallots. They resemble garlic but have a firm brown skin. The purple-skinned variety are known as Asian eschalots.

# TANDOORI PEANUT CHICKEN SKEWERS WITH SPICED POTATOES

SERVES 4

*1 cup Greek-style yoghurt* ♥
*1/3 cup tandoori paste*
*1/4 cup crunchy peanut butter*
*1 tablespoon apple cider vinegar*
*8 chicken thigh fillets, trimmed*

SPICED POTATOES

*1kg desiree potatoes, unpeeled*
*2 tablespoons olive oil*
*2 teaspoons yellow mustard seeds*
*1 teaspoon fennel seeds*
*2 teaspoons ground cumin*
*2 teaspoons ground coriander*
*2 teaspoons garam masala*
*1 teaspoon sweet paprika*
*1 teaspoon ground turmeric*
*20g butter*

1 Combine the yoghurt, tandoori paste, peanut butter and vinegar in a medium ceramic bowl. Cut chicken into pieces and stir into the tandoori mixture until well coated. Cover and refrigerate 1 hour or overnight if time permits.

2 For the spiced potatoes, cut the potatoes into 3cm pieces. Place into a saucepan and cover with cold water. Bring to the boil over high heat. Reduce heat to medium and boil gently for 5–8 minutes until potatoes are just tender when tested with a skewer. Drain well, return potatoes to the pan and shake over low heat for 1 minute.

3 Heat the oil in a large non-stick frying pan over medium heat. Add mustard seeds and fennel seeds and cook 1 minute until they start to pop. Add the remaining spices and cook, stirring 2–3 minutes until aromatic. Add the potatoes and butter and cook, tossing gently in spices for 15 minutes until the potatoes start to crisp.

4 Preheat barbecue plate on medium-high heat. Thread the marinated chicken onto 8 skewers. Grease the plate well and barbecue the skewers for 8–10 minutes, turning occasionally until cooked through. Serve with spiced potatoes and dressed salad leaves.

♥ *If time allows, spoon the yoghurt into a sieve lined with muslin and rest over a bowl, cover and refrigerate for 60 minutes to allow some moisture to drain off and the yoghurt to thicken.*

# BARBECUED LEG OF LAMB

*This is my gorgeous dad's trademark dish. He cooks it to perfection and is always proud when it hits the table.*

SERVES 4–6

*1.25kg easy-carve lamb leg, boned* ✿
*2 lemons*
*¼ cup olive oil*
*3 teaspoons smoked paprika*
*4 garlic cloves, crushed*
*2 sprigs rosemary, leaves removed*
*eggplant relish, to serve (see recipe page 47)*

1 Using a sharp knife, butterfly the lamb open to create even thickness. Turn the lamb skin side up and score the skin in a crisscross pattern. Season both sides of lamb with salt and freshly ground pepper.

2 Juice 1 lemon and thinly slice the other. Pour the juice into a large, shallow ceramic dish. Add oil, paprika and garlic and whisk to combine. Add the lamb and turn to coat. Cover and refrigerate for up to 3 hours. Remove from the fridge 30 minutes before cooking.

3 Preheat barbecue plate on medium-high heat. Add the lemon slices and lamb, skin side down, and cook for 5 minutes or until lightly charred. Remove the lemon to a plate, turn the lamb and cook a further 5 minutes until well sealed. Reduce the heat to medium-low.

4 Place a rack on the barbecue plate, set the lamb on the rack and top with rosemary and lemon slices. Close the barbecue hood ♥ and barbecue for a further 15–18 minutes for medium or until cooked to your liking.

5 Remove the lamb to a tray, cover loosely and set aside for 20–30 minutes to rest. Slice the lamb across the grain and serve with eggplant relish.

✿ When buying the lamb, ask your butcher to butterfly it open for you.

♥ If you don't have a barbecue with a hood, turn a large roasting pan or large foil roasting tray upside down over the lamb. Alternatively, transfer the lamb to the oven to complete cooking.

# SESAME-CRUSTED PORK CUTLETS WITH RED SALAD

SERVES 4

*2 tablespoons honey*
*1 tablespoon Dijon mustard*
*4 pork loin cutlets, trimmed*
*2 tablespoons sesame seeds*
*3 teaspoons yellow mustard seeds*
*2 tablespoons olive oil*

RED SALAD

*1/3 cup cranberry or pomegranate juice*
*1/2 cup dried cranberries* ✿
*1/2 red cabbage, finely shredded*
*3 pink lady apples, cored, very thinly sliced*
*1/2 cup flat-leaf parsley, chopped*
*2 tablespoons apple cider vinegar*
*1/2 cup extra-virgin olive oil*
*2 teaspoons Dijon mustard*
*2/3 cup walnuts, toasted*

1 For the red salad, bring the cranberry or pomegranate juice to the boil in a small saucepan over high heat. Remove from heat, add cranberries and set aside for 30 minutes to cool.

2 Combine the cabbage, apples and parsley in a large bowl. Pour over the cranberries and any juice. Whisk vinegar, oil, mustard, and salt and pepper together until well combined. Pour over the salad, add the walnuts and toss to combine.

3 Combine the honey and mustard in a bowl. Brush over both sides of the pork. Sprinkle the sesame and mustard seeds over both sides of the pork. Preheat the oven to 180°C fan-forced/200°C no fan.

4 Heat the oil in a large frying pan over medium-high heat. Add 2 pork cutlets, cook for 2–3 minutes or until golden, then turn and cook a further 2 minutes. Remove pork to an oven tray. Repeat with remaining cutlets. Place the cutlets into the oven and cook 5 minutes or until just cooked through. Cover and allow to rest 5 minutes. Pour a little water into the hot frying pan and stir to dissolve the bits on the base of the pan.

5 Pile salad onto plates, top with pork and spoon over a little of the pan juices.

✿ *Dried cranberries are also known as Craisins – it's a brand thing!*

# LEMONGRASS PRAWN WONTONS IN FRAGRANT BROTH

*These wontons are absolutely delicious served deep-fried (see image page 4) with roasted garlic aioli or chilli jam (see recipe pages 38 & 206).*

SERVES 4 AS LIGHT MAIN

*4 green onions, trimmed, chopped*
*2 large garlic cloves, crushed*
*3cm piece fresh ginger, peeled, chopped*
*1 stick lemongrass, chopped*
*750g green prawns, peeled, deveined, chopped*
*32 wonton wrappers*
*coriander leaves and thinly sliced chilli, to serve*

FRAGRANT BROTH

*4 cups chicken stock*
*4cm piece fresh ginger, thinly sliced*
*2 star-anise*
*1 long red chilli, thinly sliced*
*2 tablespoons soy sauce*

✿ To ensure the wontons seal properly, only brush the wrappers topped with prawn mixture. The wet edges need to come in contact with dry edges from the second wonton to form a firm seal.

1 Combine the green onions, garlic, ginger and lemongrass in a small food processor. Process until finely chopped. Alternatively, pound in a mortar with a pestle. Transfer to a glass or ceramic bowl. Add the chopped prawns and gently toss to combine.

2 Place 4 wonton wrappers on a clean bench. Spoon a heaped teaspoonful of prawn mixture into centre of each wonton. Lightly brush edges with cold water, then top with another wonton, ✿ pressing edges together to seal. Place in a single layer on a large tray, cover with a clean tea towel. Repeat with remaining wonton wrappers and prawn mixture.

3 Line base of 2 large steamer baskets with baking paper. Place wontons in a single layer in the baskets. Pour water into a wok until one-third full. Bring to the boil over high heat. Place baskets on top of each other over the wok, ensuring the base doesn't touch the water. Steam the wontons for 15–20 minutes, swapping the baskets after 10 minutes, or until wontons are cooked through. ♥

4 For the fragrant broth, combine the stock, ginger, star-anise, chilli and soy sauce in a wok or large saucepan, and bring to boil over high heat. Reduce heat to medium-low and simmer, uncovered, for 15 minutes. Strain the stock, discarding the solids.

5 To serve, transfer 4 wontons to each serving bowl. Ladle over the warm broth, top with coriander and chilli and serve.

♥ I prefer to steam the wontons separately as cooking wontons in the broth makes the broth go cloudy.

# BONDI FISH BURGER

*Oh, how times have changed. I grew up a stone's throw from beautiful Bondi Beach. During a recent trip down memory lane, I bought a fish burger (yes, and chips), and the simplicity of perfectly cooked crumbed fish, tartar sauce and lettuce on a soft bun was so good I had to recreate it.*

SERVES 4

*1 cup cornflakes*
*2 cups soft white breadcrumbs*
*2 tablespoons sesame seeds*
*2 eggs*
*¼ cup plain flour*
*600g snapper or flathead fillets, boned, skin removed, cut into long pieces*
*olive oil, for cooking*
*4 long rolls, split* ♥
*100g salad greens and lemon wedges, to serve*

TARTAR SAUCE

*½ cup whole egg mayonnaise*
*½ teaspoon red Tabasco sauce*
*2 gherkins, finely chopped*
*2 tablespoons flat-leaf parsley, chopped*
*2 tablespoons capers, drained, chopped*
*1 teaspoon lemon juice*

1 For the tartar sauce, combine all the ingredients in a bowl, season with salt and pepper. Cover and refrigerate until ready to serve.

2 Preheat oven to 200°C fan-forced/210°C no fan. Place a lightly greased cake rack onto a large baking tray. Process the cornflakes to crumbs. Transfer to a bowl, add the soft white breadcrumbs and sesame seeds, and mix well.

3 Whisk eggs together in a shallow bowl. Place the flour onto a plate and season with salt and pepper. Coat one piece of fish at a time in the flour, egg then breadcrumb mixture.

4 Pour enough oil into a large non-stick frying pan to cover the base and heat over medium-high heat until hot. Cook the fish in batches for 2 minutes each side or until light golden. Transfer to the rack. Place the fish into the oven, still on the rack, to finish cooking for 5–8 minutes or until cooked through. Place bread rolls in the oven for the final 2–3 minutes to warm through.

5 Spread a little (or a lot) of the tartar sauce over the base of each roll, top with salad leaves, fish and then more tartar. Serve with crispy potato skins (see recipe page 160).

♥ The rolls need to be the soft, Vietnamese-style rolls so when you bite into the burger nothing falls out.

# BARBECUED SALMON WITH ROASTED GARLIC AIOLI

SERVES 8

*3–4kg whole Atlantic salmon, scaled, cleaned*
*2 lemons*
*8 small fresh bay leaves*
*1 bunch tarragon*
*olive oil, for cooking*
*sprigs of fresh herbs (like parsley, basil, dill)*
*extra-virgin olive oil, lemon and lime wedges, to serve*

ROASTED GARLIC AIOLI

*1 head garlic, roasted (see recipe page 168)*
*1 cup whole egg mayonnaise*
*½ cup Greek-style natural yoghurt*
*½ lemon, juiced*
*2 tablespoons chopped chives*

1 Rinse the salmon in a sink of cold water, then pat dry with paper towel, making sure to dry inside the cavity as well. Use a sharp knife to score both sides of the salmon four times along the thickest part. Cut the lemons into rounds, then cut each round in half. Place a piece of lemon and bay leaf in each score mark. Place the remaining lemon and a quarter of the tarragon in the salmon cavity. Rub salmon with olive oil and season with plenty of sea salt flakes and freshly ground black pepper. Top with remaining tarragon sprigs and fresh herbs, and secure them to the salmon with string.

2 Tear 2 large sheets of foil and place onto the bench. Top with sheets of baking paper. Place salmon in the centre of the paper then wrap to form a parcel (not too tight), folding the edges up to seal.

3 Preheat the barbecue to 200°C, turning all burners on to medium heat. ♥ Place salmon on a large cake rack so it sits flat, then place on the barbecue. Close the barbecue hood and cook, without turning, for 45–60 minutes for medium ✿ or until cooked to your liking. Continue to check the temperature gauge – it needs to hover around 200°C. Remove fish and cool to room temperature.

4 For the roasted garlic aioli, combine the roasted mashed garlic with remaining ingredients, taste and season with salt and pepper. Cover and refrigerate until ready to serve.

5 Arrange salmon on a large platter, drizzle with extra-virgin olive oil and serve with extra lemon, lime, roasted garlic aioli and warm potato olive and caper salad (see page recipe 102).

✿ Since the size of salmon can vary, a pretty accurate guide is to allow 15 minutes per kilo for medium, with plenty of standing time.

♥ You can cook the salmon in your oven if you wish – follow the recipe, cooking it at 200°C fan-forced.

# POTATO, ROSEMARY & EGGPLANT PIZZA

SERVES 4

*2 tablespoons olive oil*
*2 garlic cloves, crushed*
*1½ cups eggplant relish (see recipe page 47)* ✿
*100g mozzarella, grated*
*20g parmesan, finely grated*
*600g desiree potatoes, thinly sliced*
*¼ cup rosemary leaves*
*baby watercress or wild rocket leaves and extra-virgin olive oil to serve*

PIZZA DOUGH

*270ml warm water*
*3 teaspoons instant dried yeast*
*1 teaspoon caster sugar*
*2 tablespoons extra-virgin olive oil*
*3 cups bread flour or plain flour*

1 Combine the olive oil and garlic together in a small bowl, cover and set aside.

2 For the pizza dough, combine the warm water, yeast, sugar, extra virgin olive oil and a pinch of salt in a large bowl. Add the flour and mix well. Knead on a lightly floured surface for 8 minutes, until elastic. Cover and set aside for 15 minutes. Preheat oven and two large flat trays to 220°C fan-forced/230°C no fan.

3 Cut the dough into 4 pieces and roll each one out on a sheet of baking paper to a rectangle roughly 12cm wide x 35cm long. Spread the eggplant relish over the base of each piece of dough. Combine the mozzarella and parmesan, and sprinkle over the relish.

4 Place the sliced potatoes onto a microwave-safe plate, cover with damp paper towel and microwave for 3 minutes on High/100%. Layer the warm potatoes over the pizzas, then scatter over the rosemary leaves. Brush the top with the garlic oil.

5 Quickly lift the pizzas (still on the baking paper) onto the hot trays and cook for 10–15 minutes or until golden and crisp. Scatter with watercress or rocket leaves, drizzle with extra-virgin oil and serve.

✿ You can replace the eggplant relish with purchased or home-made eggplant dip.

# PORK & FENNEL PASTA

*Summer is when capsicums are at their best. Combine them with pork sausage, tomatoes and pasta – perfecto!*

SERVES 4–6

*2 medium carrots, trimmed*
*2 stalks celery, trimmed*
*1 red capsicum, seeds and membrane removed*
*1 yellow capsicum, seeds and membrane removed*
*1 small red onion*
*1 long green chilli*
*¼ cup extra-virgin olive oil*
*1 tablespoon fennel seeds, bruised* ✿
*600g quality pork sausages*
*400g can whole peeled tomatoes*
*1 cup cold tap water*
*400g dried pasta (like rigatoni or orecchiette)*
*¼ cup flat-leaf parsley, chopped*
*extra-virgin olive oil and grated parmesan, to serve*

1 Roughly chop the carrots, celery, capsicum, onion and chilli, and place in a food processor. Process until finely chopped.

2 Heat the oil in a deep, large non-stick frying pan over medium-low heat. Add the fennel seeds and cook for 2 minutes or until aromatic. Add all the chopped vegetables, increase the heat to medium, and cook for 10 minutes or until soft.

3 Meanwhile, use kitchen scissors to split the casings on each sausage. Remove the sausage meat and discard the casings. Finely chop the sausage meat and add to the frying pan. Increase heat to medium-high and cook, stirring often, for 10 minutes until the pork sausage is coloured. Add the tomatoes and water, and simmer uncovered for 5–8 minutes until the sauce thickens.

4 Cook the pasta in a large saucepan of boiling salted water, following packet directions, until al dente. Drain, reserving ⅓ cup of the cooking water. Add the pasta to the sauce and toss until well coated, adding the pasta water to loosen up the sauce if necessary. Stir through the parsley, season with salt and freshly ground black pepper. Drizzle with olive oil, top with parmesan and serve.

✿ To get maximum flavour from whole spices it's a good idea to bruise them. Place in a mortar and pound gently with a pestle until you can smell the aroma. Alternatively, crush on a board with a large cook's knife.

# ROASTED TOMATO & MOZZARELLA SALAD

*This classic combination is the star attraction at any barbecue over summer, when we have a large selection of tomato varieties to choose from.*

SERVES 6 AS SIDE DISH

*2 tablespoons extra-virgin olive oil*
*1 teaspoon caster sugar*
*1 garlic clove, crushed*
*600g cherry tomatoes*
*3 buffalo mozzarella, drained, sliced*
*¼ cup small basil leaves*

PINE NUT DRESSING

*3 tablespoons extra-virgin olive oil*
*1 tablespoon red wine vinegar*
*1 teaspoon Dijon mustard*
*¼ teaspoon caster sugar*
*2 tablespoons pine nuts, toasted, chopped*

1 Combine the extra virgin olive oil, sugar, garlic, and salt and pepper in a large bowl. Add the tomatoes and toss to coat.

2 Preheat the oven and a large roasting pan to 230°C fan-forced/240°C no fan. Remove the hot pan from the oven, line the base with a sheet of baking paper, then spoon tomato mixture into the hot pan. Roast for 5 minutes until tomato skins just start to split. Remove from the oven and set aside to cool in the pan for 30 minutes.

3 For the pine nut dressing, combine all the ingredients together in a screw-top jar with salt and pepper and shake until well combined.

4 Arrange the mozzarella onto a platter, then top with tomatoes and any juices from the pan. Scatter over the basil leaves. Pour over the dressing just before serving.

# EGGPLANT RELISH

*This relish has become a real favorite since writing this recipe. Open my fridge door and you will see a jar – it goes with almost everything.*

MAKES 4 CUPS

*1kg (3 medium) eggplant*
*2 teaspoons sea salt flakes*
*½ cup olive oil*
*3 large garlic cloves, peeled, thinly sliced*
*2 long green chillies, finely chopped*
*1 red onion, finely chopped*
*1 large red capsicum, deseeded, coarsely chopped*
*2 tablespoons apple cider vinegar*
*1 tablespoon white sugar*
*⅓ cup kalamata olives, pitted, coarsely chopped* ✿
*¼ cup flat-leaf parsley, chopped*

1 Cut the eggplant into 2–3cm pieces and place on a board. Sprinkle lightly with salt and turn to coat, then transfer to a colander. Place a plate on top of the eggplant and set aside over a bowl at room temperature for 10 minutes. ♥ Rinse the eggplant well under cold running water, then drain and pat dry with paper towel.

2 Pour the olive oil into a deep, large non-stick frying pan. Add the garlic, chilli and onion and place over medium-low heat. Cook, stirring occasionally, for 15 minutes or until soft. Add the eggplant, capsicum, vinegar and sugar. Cover and cook, stirring occasionally to prevent the relish from sticking to the base of the pan, for 40–50 minutes or until the eggplant has softened and the relish is thick.

3 Stir through the olives and parsley. Set aside to cool to room temperature. Taste and then season with salt and pepper. Spoon into cold sterilised jars, label and refrigerate for up to 1 month. (Mine never lasts that long.) The relish is delicious served as a dip, spooned onto a toasted baguette or piled onto burgers, sandwiches, wraps and pizzas. (See pizza recipe page 40.)

✿ I prefer to buy olives with the seeds in – they taste better. To remove the seeds, place one olive at a time onto a board and press firmly against it, using with the palm of your hand against the flat of a large cook's knife. The olive will split, releasing the seed.

♥ Salting the eggplant in step 1 is only necessary if the eggplant has lots of large black seeds when you cut into it. This process removes the bitterness.

# CAESAR SALAD DRESSING

*This is a great dressing to master – you will never return to store-bought ones after you have tried the real thing. You can create so many variations for different salads from this one recipe.*

MAKES ¾ CUP

*1 free-range egg, from the fridge*
*1 tablespoon red wine vinegar*
*2 teaspoons Dijon mustard*
*1 anchovy fillet, chopped*
*pinch caster sugar*
*½ garlic clove, crushed*
*½ cup olive oil*

1 Bring a small saucepan of lightly salted water to the boil over high heat. Lower the egg in its shell into the water and cook for 30 seconds. Use a slotted spoon to remove the egg from the water, then run under cold water, working quickly to crack the egg into the bowl of a small food processor. ✿

2 Add the red wine vinegar, mustard, anchovy, sugar and garlic and process until well combined. With the processor on, add the oil in a slow, steady stream until the dressing is thick. Taste and season with salt and pepper.

VARIATIONS

*Creamy sesame dressing:* replace the mustard with 2 teaspoons tahini paste and stir in 1 tablespoon toasted sesame seeds at end of step 2.

*Herb dressing:* replace the red wine vinegar with apple cider vinegar and stir though 2 tablespoons chopped fresh herbs, like parsley, basil or tarragon, at end of step 2.

*Honey-mustard dressing:* increase the mustard to 2 tablespoons and replace the sugar with 2 teaspoons honey.

The dressing will keep 2–3 weeks in the fridge. The consistency of the dressing will be determined by how quickly you add the oil, and the capacity and power of the processor. You can thin it out by adding warm water.

✿ A small, 1-cup capacity food processor is a great investment for the kitchen.

# SUMMER SWEET

# SPLICE CUPS

MAKES 10

*4 limes, juiced*
*1/3 cup caster sugar*
*1 cup unsweetened pineapple juice*
*1/3 cup Greek-style yoghurt*
*1 litre quality vanilla ice-cream (Blue Ribbon brand)*
*½ cup coconut cream or milk*
*½ cup desiccated coconut*

1 Combine ½ cup of lime juice and caster sugar in a small saucepan over low heat. Stir for 5 minutes until the sugar has dissolved. Pour into a jug, add the pineapple juice and set aside to cool for 20 minutes. Whisk in the yoghurt. ♥

2 Pour about ¼ cup pineapple mixture into base of ten plastic cups. Cover and freeze 2 hours or until firm.

3 Spoon ice-cream into a large bowl and stand at room temperature until softened slightly. Stir in the coconut cream and coconut. Spoon the mixture evenly over the frozen pineapple-and-lime mixture. Cover and freeze for 30 minutes, then insert a paddle-pop stick firmly into the centre of each. Cover and freeze overnight.

4 Squeeze the plastic cups to remove the ice-pops and serve.

VARIATION

For passionfruit splice cups, replace the lime juice with fresh passionfruit pulp and omit the food colouring.

♥ *You can add a few drops of green food colouring to the mixture at this point to intensify the colour.*

# NECTARINE SHORTCAKE

*This is one of those quick, easy sweets that seriously takes little work for maximum praise.*

SERVES 6

*1 tablespoon ground almonds*
*2 tablespoons white sugar*
*2 tablespoons peach or nectarine jam (see recipe page 67)*
*3 nectarines, peeled, halved, stone removed* ♥
*icing sugar, to serve*
*double cream or vanilla ice-cream, to serve*

SHORTCAKE PASTRY

*1½ cups plain flour*
*⅓ cup caster sugar*
*100g butter, chilled, cubed*

1 For the shortcake pastry, combine the flour, caster sugar and butter in a food processor. Process until mixture resembles fine breadcrumbs. Add ¼ cup chilled water and process until the dough comes together. Turn onto a lightly floured surface and knead lightly until the base is smooth. Shape into a rectangle. If it's a warm day, wrap in greaseproof paper and refrigerate 15–20 minutes until firm enough to roll out.

2 Preheat oven and a large flat baking tray to 200°C fan-forced/210°C no fan. Roll the pastry out between 2 sheets of baking paper to form a 24cm x 32cm rectangle. Remove the top sheet of baking paper. Cut the pastry in half lengthways so you have two pieces 12cm wide, 32cm long.

3 Combine the almonds and 1 tablespoon of the white sugar in a small bowl. Spread the jam over the base of one piece of pastry. Sprinkle over the almond mixture. Place nectarines down the centre of the pastry, on top of the almond mixture, cut side down. Top with the other half of the pastry, pressing the edges together and rolling them upwards to secure.

4 Brush the top of the pastry with water and sprinkle with remaining white sugar. Cut slits 3cm apart over the top of the pastry. ✿ Leaving the shortcake on the piece of baking paper, slide it onto the hot tray. Bake for 30–35 minutes or until pastry is golden and crisp. Set aside for 10 minutes to cool slightly. Dust with icing sugar and serve warm with cream or ice-cream.

✿ This helps excess steam escape, keeping pastry crisp.

♥ I don't mind leaving the nectarine skin on in this recipe, but if you prefer to peel stone fruit, cut a small cross in the base of each piece of fruit. Place in a single layer in a large saucepan. Cover with boiling water and stand for 3 minutes. Carefully remove the fruit with a slotted spoon to a board. Use a small sharp knife to peel the skin, starting from where you cut the cross.

# BERRY CUSTARD SLICE

*This is a great recipe to use those berries that you've had in the fridge one day too long.*

MAKES 16 PIECES

*200g butter, softened*
*¾ cup caster sugar*
*1½ cups plain flour, sifted*
*½ cup ground almonds*
*450g fresh mixed berries*
*2 eggs*
*2 egg yolks*
*1 tablespoon cornflour*
*400ml thickened cream*
*200ml milk*
*1 tablespoon white sugar*

1 Preheat oven to 170°C fan-forced/180°C no fan. Grease and line a 3cm-deep, 24cm x 29cm (base) slab pan.

2 Using an electric mixer, beat butter and ½ cup of the caster sugar until well combined. Stir in the flour and almonds. Press the mixture evenly over the base of the prepared pan using a large metal spoon. Bake for 12–15 minutes or until the base is light golden. Remove from oven and set aside to cool for 10 minutes.

3 Scatter the berries over the lukewarm base. Whisk the eggs, egg yolks, cornflour and remaining ¼ cup sugar with a balloon whisk until well combined. Stir in the combined cream and milk. ✿ Strain the custard through a sieve over the berries. Return to the oven and bake a further 30 minutes or until the centre is set. Allow to cool completely in the pan.

4 Sprinkle with white sugar, cut into pieces and serve.

✿ Don't whisk with a heavy hand at this stage – too much air in the custard causes the filling to rise and fall, producing large air bubbles in the baked filling.

# AMARETTI ROASTED PEACHES

*During summer, when peaches, nectarines and plums are plentiful, make a double batch of these and just keep them in the fridge for a snack. They are great for picnics and lunch boxes, as well as dessert.*

SERVES 4

*6 freestone peaches, halved, stones removed*
*150g Amaretti biscuits* ♥
*½ cup pistachio kernels*
*1 large orange, rind finely grated, juiced*
*3 tablespoons brown sugar*
*1 egg, lightly beaten*
*double cream or vanilla ice-cream, to serve*

1 Preheat oven to 180°C fan-forced/200°C no fan. Lightly grease a large shallow baking dish. Arrange peaches in a single layer, cut side up in the dish.

2 Combine the Amaretti, pistachio, orange rind and brown sugar in a food processor. Process to fine crumbs. Transfer to a bowl and add egg. Mix until well combined. Press the mixture evenly between the peach halves.

3 Pour over the orange juice and roast, uncovered, for 15 minutes or until the top is light golden. Serve warm or cold with cream or ice-cream.

♥ Amaretti are almond macaroons. If you can't find Amaretti, you can use gingersnap or chocolate ripple.

# CHOCOLATE HAZELNUT ICE-CREAM CAKE

*If you are looking for something special to serve over summer, look no further. This is a variation of a recipe given to me by my mum's best friend, Rhonda. The applause you get when you serve this cake is well worth the effort. I make one twice this size for Christmas every year.*

SERVES 18

*150g plain chocolate biscuits (like chocolate ripple)*
*125g hazelnuts, roasted*
*150g quality dark chocolate, broken into squares (Plaistowe brand)*
*1/3 cup roasted coffee beans*
*2 litres espresso or coffee ice-cream*
*2 litres vanilla ice-cream (Blue Ribbon brand)*

CHOCOLATE FUDGE LAYER

*300g butter, softened*
*2 cups pure icing sugar*
*6 eggs, at room temperature*
*500g quality dark chocolate, melted*
*60ml Kahlúa liqueur*

1 Grease and line base and sides of a 6.5cm-deep, 24cm x 34cm (base) baking dish or roasting pan with baking paper.

2 Place biscuits into a food processor and process until crushed. Transfer to a bowl. Add the hazelnuts, dark chocolate and coffee beans to processor and process until coarsely chopped. Add to the biscuits and stir to combine.

3 Remove both the coffee and vanilla ice-cream from the freezer and allow to stand 10–15 minutes to soften slightly.

4 For the chocolate fudge layer, using an electric mixer, cream butter and icing sugar together on low speed until pale. Add the eggs one at a time, mixing well before adding the next. (Don't worry if the mixture curdles.) Add the lukewarm chocolate then the liqueur to butter mixture and beat on very low speed until just combined.

5 Spoon half of the biscuit crumb mixture over the base of the pan. Carefully spoon over half of the chocolate fudge layer and use a knife to spread so it covers the base. Spoon over the coffee ice-cream, taking care not to disturb the chocolate mixture too much. Smooth the surface then spoon over the vanilla ice-cream. Spread the remaining chocolate fudge over the ice-cream, then sprinkle over the remaining biscuit crumb mixture. Cover with plastic wrap, then two tight layers of foil and freeze for at least 24 hours, though it will keep in the freezer for up to 4 weeks.

# BRÛLÉE MANGO CHEEKS WITH FOUNDATION BISCUITS

SERVES 4

*4 large ripe mangoes*
*¼ cup Marsala (or Kahlúa)*
*½ cup white sugar* ♥
*4 passionfruit, halved*

FOUNDATION BISCUITS
MAKES 60

*250g butter, softened*
*1 cup pure icing sugar*
*1 teaspoon vanilla extract*
*¼ cup cornflour*
*2¼ cups plain flour, sifted*
*½ cup coffee crystals*

♥ Regular white sugar is coarser than caster sugar and produces a thicker, more stable toffee.

1 For the foundation biscuits, using an electric mixer, beat the butter, icing sugar and vanilla until pale. Add the cornflour and plain flour and beat on low speed until the dough just starts to come together. Using floured hands, bring the dough together and transfer to a lightly floured surface.

2 Divide the dough into four. Roll each into a log about 2½ cm wide, 15 cm long. Spread coffee crystals onto a sheet of baking paper and roll each log in the crystals until coated. Wrap each log individually in baking paper, twist ends to secure and refrigerate 30 minutes or until firm.

3 Preheat oven to 160°C fan-forced/170°C no fan. Line three trays with baking paper. Cut logs into 1cm-thick rounds. Place onto trays and bake 15–18 minutes until light golden around the edges. Allow to cool completely on trays.

4 Preheat a clean barbecue plate or large shallow non-stick frying pan on medium-high heat. Cut the cheeks from the mango stone. Score the flesh in a diamond pattern. Pour the Marsala into a shallow dish and the white sugar onto a plate.

5 Dip the cut side of the mango cheeks into the Marsala, then press into the sugar. Cut a sheet of baking paper to fit the base of the barbecue plate or pan. Place the paper on the hot barbecue plate or in the pan and add half the mangoes, cut side down. Cook for 2 minutes until sugar begins to melt. Carefully lift mangoes one at a time from the heat and press into the white sugar again. Return to the barbecue or pan and cook for a further 3 minutes or until sugar is golden.

6 Repeat with remaining mango, Marsala and sugar. (You may need a clean sheet of baking paper.) Drizzle the mangoes with passionfruit pulp and serve warm or at room temperature with foundation biscuits.

# FUDGY CHOCOLATE CHESTNUT ROULADE

*This was one of the desserts I use to supply to Station Master's Cottage Restaurant. It is simply divine – this one was polished off within minutes of us shooting this stunning image.*

SERVES 6

*5 x 60g eggs, at room temperature*
*1 cup caster sugar*
*1 teaspoon vanilla extract*
*200g quality dark chocolate, melted (Plaistowe brand)*
*1 tablespoon self-raising flour*
*300ml thickened cream*
*2 tablespoons pure icing sugar*
*¾ cup chestnut spread* ✿
*cocoa powder, for serving*

✿ Chestnut spread is a sweet mixture available in cans from the specialty section of large supermarkets or delis. Chestnut puree is unsweetened but can be turned into a spread by beating ¾ cup chestnut puree with ¾ cup pure icing sugar. You can also flavour the cream with coffee or smashed raspberries.

1 Preheat oven to 170°C fan-forced/180°C no fan. Grease and line the base and sides of a 2cm-deep, 25cm x 37cm (base) Swiss roll pan with baking paper.

2 Using an electric mixer, beat eggs, sugar and vanilla on high speed for 5–8 minutes, depending on the power of your mixer, until thick and pale. Fold in the warm melted chocolate, then the flour until just combined. Carefully spread into the pan and bake for 12–15 minutes until top is firm to touch.

3 Place a sheet of baking paper over the top of the hot roulade, then cover with a clean tea towel and turn onto the bench top. Remove the Swiss roll pan and cover the cake with another clean tea towel. Set aside to cool completely.

4 Remove the tea towel, then carefully peel off the baking paper.

5 Whip cream until thick. Fold in the icing sugar and chestnut spread. Trim the edges of the roulade, then spread with chestnut cream. Starting with the short end closest to you, roll the cake up, using the paper underneath to help. Place onto a platter and refrigerate for 6 hours or overnight if time permits.

6 Dust with cocoa powder then slice with a serrated knife to serve.

# COCONUT FRUIT BREAD

*I never skip breakfast, but there are some mornings I just have to get up and go. That's when I grab a slice of coconut fruit bread from the freezer. Quickly toasted, it's easy to eat in the car on the way to work.*

SERVES 10

*75g dried peach, chopped*
*50g dried apple, chopped*
*150ml boiling water*
*1¾ cups desiccated coconut*
*1 cup raw or white caster sugar*
*1⅔ cups self-raising flour, sifted*
*1 teaspoon ground cinnamon*
*400ml coconut milk*
*100ml milk* ✿
*1 egg, lightly beaten*
*¼ cup mixed seeds*

PEACH & PASSIONFRUIT JAM
MAKES 3 CUPS

*1kg (about 8) freestone yellow peaches, peeled (see tip page 54)*
*1½ cups white sugar*
*2 lemons, juiced*
*3 passionfruit, halved*

✿ You can replace the milk with 1 large mashed banana.

1 Combine the dried peaches and apple in a heat-proof bowl, pour the boiling water over fruit and let stand 5 minutes until soft.

2 Preheat oven to 160°C fan-forced/170°C no fan. Grease and line base and sides of a 6cm-deep, 11cm x 20cm (base) loaf pan.

3 Combine the coconut, sugar, flour and cinnamon in a large bowl. Make a well in the centre, pour in the coconut milk, milk and egg and stir until just combined. Fold in the dried fruit and any water left in the bowl, then stir in half the mixed seeds. Spread mixture into loaf pan and smooth the surface. Sprinkle the top with remaining seeds.

4 Bake for 1 hour or until a skewer inserted into the centre comes out clean. Stand in the pan for 15 minutes before lifting out onto a wire rack to cool.

5 For the peach and passionfruit jam, roughly chop the peaches and place into a 3-litre capacity heat-proof microwave-safe bowl (such as Pyrex). Add the sugar and lemon juice. Microwave, uncovered, for 4 minutes on High/100%. Stir to dissolve the sugar. Microwave, uncovered, for a further 30–35 minutes on High/100%, stirring every 10 minutes or until setting point is reached. ♥ Stir in the passionfruit pulp. Ladle the hot jam into hot sterilised jars, seal and turn upside down for 2 minutes. Turn upright and allow to cool. Once opened, store in fridge for up to 3 months.

6 Serve coconut fruit bread toasted with jam.

♥ To test for the setting point, place 1 teaspoon of jam onto a chilled saucer. Place into freezer for 2 minutes or until jam is at room temperature. Run your finger through jam – if the surface wrinkles and the jam stays in two separate portions, it's ready to bottle. If not, cook for a little longer and re-test.

# LYCHEE SPRITZER WITH SALT AND LIME PEPPER CRISPS

*Alcoholic version or not, this spritzer is the perfect way to end a hot summer's day and perfect for summer entertaining.*

SERVES 8

*2 x 565g cans lychees*
*1½ cups white sugar*
*6 limes, juiced*
*1 litre apple juice or ginger beer, chilled to serve*
*crushed ice, to serve*

SALT AND LIME PEPPER CRISPS

*3 tablespoons sea salt flakes*
*1 teaspoon black peppercorns*
*2 limes, rind finely grated*
*3 large sebago potatoes, peeled*

1 Drain the lychees, pouring the juice into a saucepan. Add the white sugar and bring to the boil over medium-high heat, stirring until the sugar has dissolved. Boil gently for 8–10 minutes or until the syrup has reduced to 1 cup. Remove from the heat. Stir in the lime juice and set aside to cool for 1 hour.

2 Combine lychee fruit and lychee and lime syrup into a blender and blend until smooth. Pour into a container and freeze overnight.

3 Scoop the frozen lychee mixture into two jugs. Pour 2 cups apple juice into each jug and stir gently to combine, then top with crushed ice. Pour into chilled glasses and serve immediately with the crisps.

4 To make the salt and pepper crisps, combine the salt, peppercorns and lime rind in a mortar and use pestle to pound until crushed and well combined, then transfer mixture to a small bowl. Using a mandolin, thinly slice the potatoes into a bowl. Pat dry with paper towel. Deep-fry potatoes in hot oil in small batches until light golden, then remove to a wire rack and sprinkle with salt and lime pepper immediately.

ADULTS-ONLY VERSION

Stir 250ml chilled vodka into the mixture after blending in step 2.

# AUTUMN

*Shorter days, cooler nights, golden leaves scattering the ground signifies summer has gone and autumn is here. It's a great time to spend a little – or a lot – more time in the kitchen.*

# BEST BUYS

## FRUIT

### MARCH

*apples:*
- *Jonathan, Gala*

*bananas*
*berries:*
- *raspberries*

*figs*
*grapes:*
- *Thompson, Crimson Seedless, Flame*

*kiwi fruit*
*limes*
*mangoes:*
- *Calypso*

*melons:*
- *rockmelon, honeydew and watermelon*

*oranges:*
- *Valencia*

*passionfruit*
*pears:*
- *Williams, Red Sensation*

*plums*
*quince*

### APRIL

*apples:*
- *Jonathan, Gala*

*bananas*
*berries:*
- *strawberries*

*custard apples*
*figs*
*grapefruit:*
- *yellow, pink and ruby red*

*grapes:*
- *Thompson, Crimson Seedless*

*limes*
*mandarins*
*nashi pears*
*papayas*
*pears:*
- *Beurre Bosc, Packham, Corella*

*persimmons*
*pomegranates*
*quince*
*tamarillos*

### MAY

*apples:*
- *Golden Delicious, Granny Smith, Jazz, Pink Lady*

*bananas*
*custard apples*
*dates*
*grapefruit*
*grapes:*
- *Thompson, Red Globe*

*kiwi fruit*
*lemons:*
- *Myer, Lisbon*

*mandarins:*
- *Imperial*

*nashi pears*
*oranges:*
- *navel*

*passionfruit*
*pears:*
- *Beurré Bosc, Packham*

*pomegranates*
*quince*

# VEGETABLES

## MARCH

*Asian greens*
*avocados:*
*Shepard*
*beans:*
*flat and green*
*cabbage:*
*red*
*capsicum:*
*red and green*
*carrots*
*chillies*
*corn*
*cucumber*
*eggplant*
*garlic*
*ginger*
*lettuce*
*mushrooms*
*onions*
*peas:*
*green*
*potatoes*
*pumpkin:*
*Jarrahdale*
*spinach:*
*English and baby*
*sweet potato*
*tomatoes*
*zucchini*

## APRIL

*Asian greens*
*avocados:*
*Shepard, Hass*
*beans:*
*green and snake*
*broccoli*
*brussels sprouts*
*cabbage:*
*red, savoy, plain*
*carrots*
*chillies*
*corn*
*cucumber*
*eggplant*
*fennel*
*garlic*
*ginger*
*lettuce*
*mushrooms*
*onions*
*parsnip*
*potatoes*
*pumpkin:*
*Butternut, Jarrahdale, Japanese*
*spinach:*
*English and baby*
*sweet potato*
*tomatoes*
*zucchini and squash*

## MAY

*Asian greens*
*avocados:*
*Hass, Sharwil*
*broccoli*
*brussels sprouts*
*cabbage:*
*red*
*carrots*
*cauliflower*
*celeriac*
*chillies*
*corn*
*eggplant*
*fennel*
*garlic*
*ginger*
*Jerusalem artichokes*
*leek*
*mushrooms*
*onions*
*parsnip*
*potatoes*
*pumpkin:*
*Japanese*
*silverbeet*
*sweet potato*
*turnip*
*zucchini and squash*

# PRODUCE

## BANANAS

The most common varieties in Australia are the Cavendish and the Lady Finger, though keep an eye out for a new variety called Gold Finger – they don't brown when they are cut.

*Storage*: Store at room temperature, out of direct sunlight. Once ripe, bananas can be kept in the fridge – their skin will turn black but the fruit inside is fine. Bananas can be frozen in their skin. Once thawed, the flesh will be soft so it's best used for baking.

*Tip:* Keep bananas away from avocados, apples and kiwi fruit as these release ethylene gas, which accelerates ripening.

*Best buddies with:* Yoghurt, cream and ice-cream, caramel, maple syrup, honey, cinnamon and chocolate.

## APPLES

With close to 10,000 varieties grown world wide, it's easy to understand why we get confused when we see new varieties on our shelves each year.

*Best apple to cook for puree:* Granny Smith, Braeburn, Royal Gala
*Best baking apple:* Golden Delicious and Fuji
*Best apple in salad:* Pink Lady and Sundowner
*Best eating apple:* Pink Lady, Red Delicious, Jonathan and Gala
*Best apple to juice:* Granny Smith

Keep an eye out for a new variety called Jazz. It's crisp, sweet and juicy – the perfect eating apple.

*Storage:* Apples keep their crispness and stay fresh for longer when stored loosely in the fridge crisper.

*Best buddies with:* Butter, cream, white and brown sugar, honey, golden syrup and maple syrup, cinnamon, vanilla, cheese, eggs, duck.

## FIGS

They have two seasons, making a brief appearance in early summer with the bumper crop traditionally in autumn.

*Storage:* Firm fruit will ripen within 1–2 days at room temperature or 3–4 days if kept in the fridge. Store ripe fruit loosely covered with plastic on a plate in a single layer in the coldest part of the fridge for up to 2 days.

*Tip:* For maximum flavour, always serve at room temperature. The entire fig is edible from the skin to the red or purplish flesh and the tiny seeds.

*Best buddies with:* Almost any kind of nut, walnuts being the pick; honey, pancetta, prosciutto, ham and bacon; capers and olives; cinnamon, nutmeg, star-anise and cloves; oranges, cream, mascarpone and crème fraîche; firm or soft blue cheese; rum and port.

## ASIAN GREENS

These have become as common as carrots and peas on our dinner plate, but their changing names and uses over the years has caused confusion.

Choy sum has slender stems, like English spinach, with edible yellow flowers. It has a mild flavour and is perfect for adding to soups and stir-fry as the stems are of even thickness.

Gai lan (Chinese broccoli) has edible white flowers and thicker stems than choy sum. It is related to broccoli and kale, and is best stir-fried, sautéed, pan-fried or steamed.

Pak choy and bok choy are basically the same plant. Bok choy has a white stem and is bigger, and pak choy has a green stem. The baby variety of each usually comes three to the bunch and are be cooked or shredded and served raw.

Broccolini is a cross between broccoli and gai lan. The stems are asparagus-like in appearance but have tiny broccoli buds flowering at the top. It has a mild broccoli taste with a slightly peppery kick.

*Tip:* When cooking Asian greens, trim the base and separate the stalks and leaves. Cook the stems first (they take longer) and add the leaves right at the last minute so they are served as soon as they wilt.

*Storage:* Keep unwashed in a storage bag in the fridge crisper for 2–3 days.

*Best buddies with*: All things Asian: ginger; garlic; chilli; soy, oyster and kecap manis; mushrooms; snake beans; chicken, duck, prawns and pork; rice and noodles.

## MUSHROOMS

Mushrooms are one of the most versatile vegetables available and are one of the highest antioxidant foods in the world.

Buttons, cups and flats are all the one variety: the longer they are left to grow, the larger they become, actually doubling in size every 24 hours. Buttons: use raw or marinated in salads or stir-fry. Cups: great with pasta and rice dishes. Flats: use in soups, sauces or casseroles and roasted, grilled or stuffed.

Oyster mushrooms are delicate and absorb the flavours they are cooked with, so stir-fried are best.

Enoki grow in clusters, have a mild fruity flavour and a crisp texture when eaten raw. Trim the stems and separate. Use raw in salads and wraps or cooked in broths.

Swiss browns have a tan-coloured skin and their firm flesh is perfect for risotto.

Portobello are great roasted and barbecued whole.

Shiitaki have a rich flavour and 'meaty' texture. Always remove the hard, woody stem. Use in braises, soups, stocks or sauces.

*Storage:* Store unwashed in brown paper bags on the lowest shelf in your fridge. They will 'sweat' in plastic bags, which leads to quick deterioration.

*Best buddies with:* Butter; olive oil; garlic, ginger and chilli; eggs, cheese, cream and yoghurt; noodles, rice and pasta; bacon, ham, chicken and beef; parsley, thyme and basil; bread.

## EGGPLANT

Also know as aubergines, eggplants are polarising – you either love them or hate them. I became a fan when I tasted baba ghanoush, a Middle Eastern dip. I progressed onto Moussaka (Greek lamb bake), parmigiana and caponata, and now eggplant is always in my fridge. Eggplant can be chargrilled, baked, stuffed, puréed, baked or pan-fried.

The skin of the eggplant is edible, so wash and dry well before slicing off the spiky green calyx. Some recipes suggest sprinkling the flesh with salt to remove the bitterness; this is know as 'degorging'. It is only necessary in large eggplants where the seeds have turned black (see page 47). This process also extracts excess moisture from eggplant, which reduces the amount of oil it soaks up when baked, grilled or fried.

*Tip*: Buy small or medium eggplant with smooth, shiny, wrinkle-free skin. They should feel heavy for their size.

*Best buddies* with: olive oil; lemon and tomato; onion and garlic; haloumi, mozzarella, bocconcini and parmesan; ground cumin and coriander; yoghurt; tahini; oregano, basil and mint; olives and capers.

## ONION

Brown onions have a strong flavour and are excellent for cooking.

White onions are milder than brown onions, though they have a pungent, peppery flavour. They can be used raw.

Red onions have a purple-red skin. The purple pigment can stop after the first layer or penetrate right through to the centre. They are quite mild and can be cooked, pickled or served raw.

Pickling onions can be of any variety. They are planted close together and harvested early to retain their size and mild flavour.

Shallots, also known as eschalot, have a golden-brown skin with slightly pinkish flesh. They are small in size with several small bulbs formed together, making them tedious to peel, but don't let this put you off. They are milder than all other dry varieties and widely used in French and Asian cuisine.

Green onions, also known as green shallots, are immature onions harvested when the tops are green and before the bulb has begun to mature.

Spring onions, also known as salad onions, are the next stage of the green onion. Left in the ground a little longer, their bulbs are semi-developed, producing a small, sweet onion. The bulb and light-green part of the stem can be used. They're great in salads, roasted until soft and golden or chopped and used in Asian dishes.

# AUTUMN SAVOURY

# BREAKFAST TORTILLA

*When I was studying, basic skills classes were always my favourites – repetitive and tedious, granted – but understanding and mastering the essentials, like scrambled eggs, opened all the other cooking doors.*

MAKES 4

*4 white flour tortillas*
*4 free-range eggs, at room temperature*
*2 tablespoons milk*
*30g butter, chopped*
*2 ripe tomatoes, quartered, seeds removed, diced*
*1 avocado, diced*
*2 green onions, thinly sliced*
*hot chilli sauce, to serve, optional*

1 Preheat the oven to 150°C fan-forced/160°C no fan. Wrap the tortillas in foil. Place in the oven for 8–10 minutes or until warm. ✿

2 Using a fork, beat the eggs and milk together vigorously for 2 minutes until the yolks and whites are well combined. (Don't add salt as it will cause the egg to weep during cooking.) Set aside for 5 minutes to allow the large air bubbles to settle.

3 Preheat a 20cm (base) non-stick frying pan over medium heat. Once hot, add the butter and swirl quickly to coat the pan. As the very last of the butter is melting, pour the eggs into the pan. Cook for 1 minute until the egg just starts to set around the edges.

4 Using a spatula or a flat-edged wooden spoon, push the set egg from the outer edge of the pan toward the centre, while tilting the pan to distribute the uncooked egg to the outer edge of the pan. Cook for a further 30–45 seconds, then remove the pan from the heat. The egg should still be soft.

5 Working with one tortilla at a time (keep the rest wrapped), spoon one-quarter of the egg onto half the tortilla. Top with tomato, avocado and green onions. Fold over to enclose the filling, then repeat to make the remaining tortillas. Serve with chilli sauce if desired.

✿ To warm tortillas in the microwave, layer them between damp paper towel. Place onto a microwave-safe plate, cover the top with damp paper towel and microwave for 45 seconds per tortilla on medium/50%.

# LAMB, SPINACH & FETA SAUSAGE ROLLS

*There is a chain in Sydney called Bourke Street Bakery, and every foodie I know raves about their sausage rolls – me included. I live too far away to satisfy that craving, so I created this recipe so we can all enjoy great sausage rolls whenever we like. Yes, they freeze raw or cooked, not that there are ever any leftovers.*

MAKES 30

*1kg lamb mince*
*6 green onions, finely chopped*
*2 cups finely shredded English spinach or silverbeet*
*1 cup soft white breadcrumbs*
*¼ cup flat-leaf parsley, chopped*
*¼ cup pine nuts, toasted, chopped*
*2 eggs*
*150g marinated feta, well drained*
*3 sheets frozen ready-rolled puff pastry, partially thawed* ♥
*tomato chutney, to serve*

1 Preheat the oven to 200°C fan-forced/220°C no fan. Line 2 large flat baking trays with baking paper.

2 Combine the mince, green onions, spinach, breadcrumbs, parsley, pine nuts and 1 egg in a large bowl. Mix with clean hands until well combined. Crumble over the feta and stir gently to combine. Season with a little salt and plenty of freshly ground black pepper.

3 Cut 1 pastry sheet in half. Beat the remaining egg with a fork. Spoon the filling in a sausage shape along the long edge closest to you. Brush the opposite long edge lightly with beaten egg. Roll up and press the pastry edges together to seal. Repeat with remaining filling and pastry.

4 Cut each roll into 5 smaller ones. Brush the top of each sausage roll with egg. Place seam side down onto trays, allowing room for spreading. Bake for 15–20 minutes or until golden and puffed. Serve hot, warm or at room temperature with tomato chutney.

♥ It's far easier working with pastry still a little frozen – just make sure it's completely thawed before you start cooking. If you are able to buy the Carême brand ready-rolled puff, do so – it's well worth it.

# SLOW-COOKED LAMB SHOULDER

*I have to tell you – summer, autumn, winter or spring – this recipe never disappoints. You can use lamb leg or even easy-carve lamb roast if you prefer.*

SERVES 6

*2 x 1.2kg lamb shoulders on the bone*
*4 garlic cloves, crushed*
*1 long red chilli, deseeded, finely chopped*
*1/3 cup ginger and lime marmalade*
*2 tablespoons olive oil*
*1 bunch thyme*
*4 cups chicken stock*
*1/3 cup dried sour cherries or Craisins*
*1/3 cup mint leaves*
*1/4 cup flat-leaf parsley*
*couscous or steamed rice, to serve*

✿ To maintain 130°C temperature on the barbecue, ignite the burner furthest from the lamb on medium-low heat. If you don't have a barbecue with a hood, follow steps 1 and 2 then cook lamb in oven on 120°C fan-forced/130°C no fan.

1 Preheat the barbecue plate on medium-high until hot, using all burners. Score the skin side of both shoulders of lamb. Combine the garlic, chilli, marmalade and 1 tablespoon of the oil in a bowl. Using half of the mixture, brush over both sides of each lamb shoulder.

2 Drizzle the remaining oil over the barbecue plate and add the lamb, skin side down. Barbecue for 5 minutes until golden and a little charred. Turn and barbecue a further 4–5 minutes until golden all over. Remove the lamb to a large plate.

3 Scrape the barbecue plate clean, close the hood and reduce the burners to low – the temperature gauge should read 130°C. ✿

4 Spread the remaining marmalade mixture over the skin side of both lamb shoulders. Place skin side up onto a rack inside a deep, large roasting pan. Scatter over the thyme and season with salt and freshly ground pepper. Pour enough stock into the pan, covering the base but not touching the lamb. Cover tightly with two layers of foil. Place the pan onto the barbecue plate, close the barbecue hood and cook for 6 hours, adding more stock every hour as it evaporates. (This provides the gravy for later.)

5 Transfer the lamb to a platter using a large spoon or spatula – it literally falls from the bone as you move it – cover and set aside to rest for 15 minutes. Pour the pan juices into a saucepan and bring to the boil. Remove from the heat, add the dried cherries or Craisins.

6 Use two forks to shred the lamb from the bone, spoon over the pan juices, then scatter over the combined mint and parsley. Serve with couscous or rice.

# SEARED BEEF WITH MUM'S ONION RICE

*This is one of my all-time favourite recipes. The beef is something I created by accident but just works, and Mum's rice – well, like everything Mum makes, it's delicious.*

SERVES 6

*2 x 600g pieces beef fillet* ✿
*olive oil*
*2 long red chillies, deseeded, chopped*
*6cm piece ginger, peeled, chopped*
*2 large garlic cloves*
*2 french eschalots, peeled, chopped*
*2 coriander roots, scraped, chopped*
*1 cup white sugar*
*1 lime, juiced*
*2 tablespoons fish sauce*
*2 tablespoons cold water*
*2 teaspoons sesame oil*

MUM'S ONION RICE

*1½ cups long-grain rice, rinsed*
*3 tablespoons olive oil*
*50g butter, chopped*
*3 brown onions, halved, chopped*
*2 teaspoons caster sugar*
*1 tablespoon garlic salt*

✿ I have used beef eye fillet, but beef scotch fillet or rolled beef rump roast also work well. Compare the prices and choose the cut that suits your budget on the day. When using scotch fillet, buy a 1.25kg piece and cut it in half lengthways to form two thinner fillets (cooking time above stands).

1 For Mum's onion rice, cook rice following absorption method on the packet. Rinse in cold water, drain well, then spread onto a tray, cover and refrigerate for 2 hours until cold. Heat the oil and butter in a large, deep, frying pan over medium-low heat. Add onions and cook, stirring often for 20 minutes until soft. Add the sugar, increase the heat to medium and cook until the onions are light golden. Stir in the rice and garlic salt and cook, gently stirring for 5 minutes until rice is warmed through.

2 Preheat the oven and a roasting pan to 200°C fan-forced/210°C no fan. Trim the sinew from the beef, then tie each beef fillet at 3cm intervals with kitchen string to help hold its shape while cooking.

3 Rub the beef all over with the oil and season well with freshly ground pepper. Heat a large non-stick frying pan over high heat until very hot. Add a little oil then the beef and cook for 3 minutes, turning to sear the beef all over, including the ends. Lightly grease the hot roasting pan and add the beef. Roast for 12 minutes, turn the beef over and roast a further 10 minutes for medium or until cooked to your liking. Remove from the oven, cover and set aside to rest for 15 minutes.

4 Meanwhile, combine chilli, ginger, garlic, eschalots and coriander root in a small food processor, and process until almost smooth. Pour the sugar into a medium saucepan. Place over medium-high heat and cook, stirring occasionally, for 5 minutes until the sugar turns golden. Combine the lime juice, fish sauce, water and sesame oil, and pour into the hot caramel (take care – the mixture may spit). Reduce heat to medium and cook, stirring until caramel dissolves again. Remove from the heat and stir in the chilli mixture. Cover to keep warm.

5 Slice the warm beef, then pour the warm sauce over the warm beef, cover and allow to stand at least 20 minutes.

6 Serve the beef with plenty of sauce and Mum's rice.

# MY CHILLI CON CARNE

*Chilli con carne translates to 'chilli with meat', I am not a fan of kidney beans, but if you want to make the meal go further, feel free to stir in a well-drained 400g can of red kidney beans in step 5 when adding the shredded beef to the sauce.*

SERVES 4

*2 chorizo sausages, ends trimmed*
*2 brown onions, chopped*
*2 garlic cloves, chopped*
*2 green jalapeños* ✿
*1kg steak (skirt, flank, gravy beef or blade), trimmed*
*3 tablespoons olive oil*
*2 teaspoons ground cumin*
*3 teaspoons hot paprika*
*1 cinnamon stick*
*2 cups beef stock*
*400g can diced tomatoes*
*2 tablespoons malt vinegar*
*1 tablespoon dried oregano*
*2 teaspoons caster sugar*
*Crispy fried tortillas, diced avocado, sour cream and lime wedges, to serve*

♥ Every kitchen should have 1 or 2 pieces of flameproof ovenware (if budget allows, a large roasting pan and a large casserole dish with a lid). You can begin cooking the dish – like a casserole, roast or risotto – on the stove top then transfer it to the oven. They come in all shapes, sizes and colours, produce brilliant results, and save you on washing-up.

1 Preheat the oven to 130°C fan-forced/130°C no fan. Roughly chop the chorizo and place in a food processor with onions, garlic and jalapeños. Process until finely chopped and set aside. Cut the beef into large pieces about 10–12cm in size.

2 Heat a large ovenproof pan ♥ over medium-high heat until very hot. Add 1 tablespoon of the oil and half the beef, cook for 5 minutes, turning the beef until browned all over, then remove to a plate. Repeat with the rest of the beef.

3 Reduce the heat to medium-low, add the remaining oil and the chorizo mixture. Cook, stirring, for 8 minutes or until light golden. Add the cumin, paprika and cinnamon stick and cook, stirring, for 1 minute until aromatic. Return the beef and any juices on the plate to the pan. Add the stock, tomatoes, vinegar, oregano and sugar and bring to a simmer. Turn the heat off and press a piece of baking paper right down onto the surface of the liquid as this will help keep the beef submerged.

4 Cover the pan with a tight-fitting lid and transfer to the oven. Cook for 4 hours. Remove the pan from the oven. Transfer the beef to a large plate, cover and stand 10 minutes. While the beef is resting, place the pan onto the stovetop and bring the tomato mixture to the boil over medium heat. Boil gently, uncovered, for 10 minutes until sauce reduces slightly.

5 Using two forks, shred the beef into strips. Remove the cinnamon stick from the sauce and stir in the beef, taste and season with salt and freshly ground black pepper. Serve with tortilla, avocado, sour cream and lime wedges.

✿ Fresh jalapeños are oval-shaped and quite spicy. If fresh ones are unavailable, you can buy them pickled in jars near where you find olives.

# CHARRED CHICKEN WITH COCONUT SALSA

*If you're looking for inspiration for the chicken fillets sitting in your fridge, you can stop here for perfect mid-week food.*

SERVES 4

*4 chicken breast fillets*
*2 tablespoons extra-virgin olive oil*
*1 lemon, juiced*
*1 teaspoon chilli flakes*
*pinch caster sugar*
*4 cobs corn, husks on*
*lemon wedges, to serve*

COCONUT SALSA

*¼ cup flaked coconut*
*1 long red chilli, seeded, finely chopped*
*1 long green chilli, seeded, finely chopped*
*3 green onions, finely chopped*
*2 tablespoons mint leaves, shredded*

1 Cut each chicken fillet in half horizontally to form two thinner fillets, and place into a ceramic bowl. Combine the oil, lemon, chilli, sugar and salt and pepper in a screw-top jar and shake until well combined. Pour over the chicken and turn to coat. Cover and refrigerate for 10 minutes (no longer than an hour).

2 Peel back the corn husks and remove the fine silk. Reposition the husks back over the corn. Soak the corn in a bowl of cold water for 5 minutes. Drain well, shaking the corn.

3 Preheat the barbecue grill on medium heat. Add corn and barbecue for 15–20 minutes, turning often, until the corn kernels are just tender. ♥ Remove the chicken from the marinade and barbecue for 3–4 minutes each side or until lightly charred and just cooked through. Transfer to a tray, cover and allow to rest for 5 minutes.

4 Combine all the coconut salsa ingredients together, spoon over the chicken, drizzle with a little oil and serve with the corn, any remaining coconut salsa and lemon wedges.

♥ To speed up the cooking, microwave the corn for 5 minutes on High/100%. It will then only need 8–10 minutes on the barbecue.

# INDIAN SPICED CHICKEN

*Indian cuisine is certainly growing in popularity – the flavours are exciting and revolve around fresh, aromatic spices.*

SERVES 4

*2 teaspoons ground cumin*
*2 teaspoons ground coriander*
*1 teaspoon garam masala*
*2 teaspoons sweet paprika*
*1 teaspoon ground fennel*
*1 teaspoon ground turmeric*
*½ teaspoon ground cinnamon*
*pinch cayenne powder*
*1 cup Greek yoghurt*
*2 garlic cloves, crushed*
*3cm-piece fresh ginger, peeled, grated*
*4 Maryland chicken pieces, skin on* ✿
*steamed basmati rice and minted yoghurt, to serve*

1 Combine all the spices in a small non-stick frying pan over medium heat. Cook, shaking the pan, for 3–4 minutes or until the spices are warm and aromatic, remove from heat and transfer to a ceramic dish straightaway. ♥ Set aside to cool. Stir the yoghurt into the cool spices then add garlic and ginger and mix well.

2 Cut 2–3 slits into thick part of the chicken leg of each Maryland, then add to the yoghurt mixture and rub with your fingertips to coat the chicken. Cover and refrigerate 1–2 hours or overnight if you wish.

3 Preheat the oven to 200°C fan-forced/210°C no fan. Place the chicken skin side up onto a large baking tray lined with baking paper. Roast the chicken for 30 minutes, increase the oven temperature to 240°C fan-forced/240°C no fan and cook for 5 minutes or until lightly charred around edges and cooked through. Stand for 5 minutes before serving with rice and yoghurt. For a well-balanced meal, serve with sautéed spinach.

✿ If you can't get chicken Maryland, you can use chicken thigh or cutlets on the bone.

♥ It's important to remove the spices from the pan. If left, the residual heat may burn the spices.

# LAKSA LEMAK

*Laksa is one of my favourite dishes when I order Thai, but it's also a regular soup I make as the weather turns cooler. Ms Dok, my Thai cooking teacher, will be thrilled I am passing her recipe along.*

SERVES 4

*250g dried rice vermicelli noodles*
*1 tablespoon peanut oil*
*½ cup laksa paste* ✿
*3 cups chicken stock*
*3 cups coconut milk*
*4 fried bean curd puffs, thickly sliced* ♥
*2 teaspoons grated palm sugar or brown sugar*
*½ lime, juiced*
*2 teaspoons fish sauce*
*50g bean sprouts, trimmed*
*1 Lebanese cucumber, peeled, cut into thin strips*
*½ cup mint leaves*
*½ cup coriander leaves*
*3 green onions, thinly sliced*
*fried shallots and lime wedges, to serve*

POACHED CHICKEN

*2 chicken breast fillets, trimmed*
*1 lime, thinly sliced*
*1 stick lemongrass, chopped*
*2cm piece galangal or ginger, thinly sliced*
*1 small red chilli, halved*

1 For the poached chicken, place the chicken into a non-stick frying pan. Pour over enough cold water to cover. Add the remaining ingredients and bring to a simmer over medium heat. Simmer, uncovered, for 15 minutes. Remove from the heat. Set aside for 15 minutes to rest in the poaching liquid, drain, then thinly slice the chicken across the grain.

2 Place the noodles in a heat-proof bowl. Cover with boiling water. Set aside for 3 minutes or until the noodles have softened slightly. Drain and set aside.

3 Heat a wok over medium heat until hot. Add the oil and swirl to coat the wok. Add the laksa paste and cook, stirring for 2 minutes or until fragrant and the oil separates from the paste. Pour in the stock and bring to the boil. Reduce heat to medium-low, add coconut milk and bean curd. Simmer for 10 minutes.

4 Add the shredded chicken. Combine the palm sugar, lime juice and fish sauce and pour into the wok, then simmer for 3 minutes until chicken is warmed through.

5 Divide the noodles among serving bowls, then ladle over the soup. Top with bean sprouts, cucumber, mint, coriander, green onions and fried shallots. Serve with lime wedges.

✿ Laksa paste can vary in flavour from mild to very hot. The authentic ones from Asian grocery stores generally have a good balance of flavour and heat.

♥ Fried bean curd puffs are available in the fridge section of Asian grocery stores. You can leave it out of the recipe if you like.

# EASY FISH STEW

*This recipe came about working with my dear friend Kate Nichols on a magazine shoot. It's totally Kate's idea, 'borrowed' with one small change – I substituted fish for chicken, since we all need to increase our consumption of fish midweek.*

SERVES 4

*2 large garlic cloves, roughly chopped*
*5cm-piece ginger, peeled, roughly chopped*
*1 long green chilli, roughly chopped*
*2 fresh coriander roots, scrubbed*
*1 stick lemongrass, pale section only, roughly chopped*
*¼ cup pistachio kernels, toasted*
*1 tablespoon peanut oil*
*2¼ cups chicken stock*
*400ml coconut milk*
*800g skinless firm white fish fillets, cut into 3cm pieces* ♥
*1 bunch Asian greens like gai lan, leaves separated, stems roughly chopped*
*2 cups cooked jasmine rice*
*6 green onions, thinly sliced*

1 Combine the garlic, ginger, chilli, coriander roots, lemongrass and pistachio kernels in a small food processor and process to a paste. Alternatively, pound in a mortar with a pestle.

2 Pour the oil into a cold wok, add the lemongrass mixture and place over medium heat. Cook, stirring, for 5–8 minutes or until you start to smell the spice mixture. Pour in the stock and coconut milk and bring to a simmer. Add the fish and Asian green stems and cook, stirring occasionally, for 5 minutes until the fish is just cooked through.

3 Shred the Asian green leaves and stir into the stew. Remove from the heat.

4 Spoon the rice into the base of shallow bowls, ladle over the stew and serve topped with green onions.

♥ Varieties of fish that work well are snapper, kingfish, red emperor.

# HAM, LEEK & CHEESE CROQUETTES

*Crispy and crunchy on the outside, soft and velvety in the centre, croquettes should be enjoyed occasionally on cool autumn or winter nights.*

MAKES 24

*150g butter, chopped*
*½ cup plain flour*
*2 cups milk*
*1 large leek, halved lengthways*
*1 tablespoon olive oil*
*100g cheddar cheese, grated*
*350g piece smoked ham, diced* ♥
*½ cup self-raising flour*
*3 eggs, lightly beaten*
*4 cups soft white breadcrumbs*
*vegetable oil, for deep-frying*
*lemon wedges, to serve*

♥ You can buy pieces of smoked ham in the meat section at supermarkets and, of course, from your local butcher – it's cheaper and keeps longer than pre-cut ham.

1 Melt the butter in a medium saucepan over medium heat until hot. Add the plain flour, cook, stirring constantly for 2 minutes or until mixture starts to bubble. ✿ Remove pan from the heat, add the milk slowly, whisking with a balloon whisk constantly until all milk has been added. Return to the heat and cook, stirring with a wooden spoon until the sauce comes to the boil. Season with salt and pepper, then spoon the sauce into a bowl and cover the surface with plastic wrap to prevent a skin forming. Refrigerate for 3–4 hours or until cold.

2 Thinly slice the leek. Heat the oil in a small saucepan over medium heat. Add the leek and cook, stirring often, for 4 minutes or until soft. Set aside to cool. Stir the leek, cheese and ham into the thick white sauce mixture. Using a heaped tablespoon of ham mixture, shape into balls.

3 Coat one croquette at a time in flour, egg and then breadcrumbs. Coat in egg and breadcrumbs a second time. (This produces a nice thick coating.) Place the croquettes onto a large tray and refrigerate for 2 hours until firm. You can leave them overnight like this if you wish.

4 Preheat the oven to 180°C fan-forced/200°C no fan. Half fill a wok, deep-fryer or large saucepan with oil and heat over medium-high heat until hot. Cook the croquettes in batches for 3–4 minutes or until golden and crisp. Transfer to a wire rack and place the rack into the oven to keep the croquettes warm while cooking remaining croquettes. Sprinkle with salt and serve warm with lemon wedges.

✿ If the flour isn't cooked long enough or the milk is added too quickly, your sauce may become lumpy. Don't panic – pour the sauce into a sieve and use a wooden spoon to push the sauce through and continue.

# CHAR-SIU PORK

*I have used pork fillet, since it's more widely available, though this recipe traditionally uses pork Scotch fillet or pork neck, which are often cheaper per kilo at Asian butchers. Be sure to cut these into 5–6cm thick strips so they resemble a fillet and cook through.*

SERVES 6

*½ cup char-siu sauce*
*4 tablespoons brown sugar*
*1 teaspoon Chinese five-spice powder*
*1/3 cup Shaoxing Chinese cooking wine* ♥
*2 (about 850g total) pork fillets, trimmed*
*1 tablespoon peanut oil*
*Asian greens, steamed to serve*
*steamed noodles or rice, to serve*

1 Combine the char-siu sauce, brown sugar, Chinese five-spice and Chinese cooking wine in a small saucepan over medium heat. Bring to a simmer, stirring often to prevent marinade sticking to the base of the pan. Reduce the heat to medium-low and cook for 3 minutes. Set aside to cool completely.

2 Spoon half the marinade into a ceramic dish, cover the rest and refrigerate until required. Add the pork to the dish and turn to coat. Cover and refrigerate for 4 hours or overnight if time permits.

3 Preheat the barbecue plate on medium heat. Remove the pork from the marinade and discard marinade. Grease the barbecue plate with oil, then barbecue the pork, turning and brushing with reserved marinade from the fridge every few minutes for 10–15 minutes or until sticky and cooked through. Remove the pork to a board, cover and stand for 15 minutes. Slice and serve with Asian greens and fresh rice noodles or steamed jasmine rice.

♥ Shaoxing Chinese cooking wine is inexpensive and available at Asian grocery stores.

# SINGAPORE NOODLES

*If you ever get the chance to visit Singapore, you must visit the food markets. Almost every street corner has a vendor selling a variation of Singapore noodles, so try them all.*

SERVES 4

*3cm-piece fresh ginger, peeled, chopped*
*1 long red chilli, chopped*
*1 stick lemongrass, chopped*
*1 tablespoon mild curry powder*
*3 tablespoons vegetable oil*
*2 eggs, lightly beaten*
*1 brown onion, halved, thinly sliced*
*2 rashers bacon, rind removed, finely chopped*
*400g cooked char-siu pork, chopped* *(see recipe page 98)* ✿
*450g fresh Singapore noodles*
*2 tablespoons dark soy sauce*
*2 tablespoons Shaoxing Chinese cooking wine*
*100g bean sprouts, trimmed*
*6 green onions, thinly sliced*
*finely chopped salted peanuts or fried shallots, to serve*

1 Combine the ginger, chilli, lemongrass, curry powder and 1 tablespoon of the oil in a small food processor and process to a paste. Alternatively, pound in a mortar with a pestle. Set aside.

2 Heat a wok over medium heat until hot. Add 2 teaspoons of the oil and swirl to coat the wok. Add the egg and swirl to form a thin omelette. Cook for 30 seconds or until the egg is almost set. Slide onto a board and roll the omelette up.

3 Add the remaining oil to the hot wok with the onion and bacon and stir-fry for 2 minutes or until the onion is just tender. Add the ginger paste and stir-fry for 30 seconds until aromatic.

4 Add the pork and stir-fry for 2 minutes or until just warmed through. Separate the noodles and add to the wok. Stir-fry for 1 minute or until noodles begin to soften. Combine the soy and cooking wine, then add to the wok with the bean sprouts and green onions. Stir-fry for 1–2 minutes or until noodles are hot. Thinly slice the omelette crossways and add to the noodles. Serve topped with peanuts or shallots.

✿ Of course, if you have a good Asian butcher or grocery store near you, you can buy pork already cooked. For those of us not that lucky, it's easy to make your own, and it's sensational.

# WARM POTATO, OLIVE & CAPER SALAD

*There are two important tips to make a potato salad great: choose the right potato and dress the potatoes while they are warm.*

SERVES 6 AS SIDE

*1kg chat, kipfler or Nicola potatoes, unpeeled*
*½ cup extra-virgin olive oil*
*2 tablespoons sherry or red wine vinegar*
*2 teaspoons Dijon mustard*
*1 teaspoon caster sugar*
*¼ cup whole egg mayonnaise or Greek-style yoghurt*
*2 tablespoons drained capers*
*¾ cup kalamata olives, pitted*
*1 small red onion, halved, very thinly sliced* ✿
*2 tablespoons pine nuts, toasted*
*¼ cup flat-leaf parsley, roughly chopped*

1 Scrub the potatoes, then place in a medium saucepan and cover with cold water. Cover with lid and bring to the boil over high heat. Remove the lid and cook for 20–30 minutes, depending on their size, or until just tender. ♥

2 Meanwhile, combine the olive oil, vinegar, mustard, sugar and salt and pepper in a screw-top jar and shake until well combined.

3 Drain the potatoes, then cut in half or in chunks and transfer to a large bowl. Pour half the dressing over the hot potatoes and stir gently to coat. Set aside for 10 minutes to allow the potatoes to absorb the dressing.

4 Add the mayonnaise to the remaining dressing, secure the lid and shake until well combined. Add the capers, olives, red onion and pine nuts to the potatoes. Pour over the mayonnaise mixture, toss gently to coat, then pile onto a platter. Scatter over the parsley and serve warm or at room temperature.

✿ If you have a mandolin, use it to finely slice the onion.

♥ Insert a toothpick or small skewer into one potato before covering with cold water. When you can remove the toothpick with little resistance, the potatoes are ready for draining.

# EGGPLANT PARMIGIANA

*Is there anything more comforting than a big spoonful of parmigiana alongside some crumbed veal? I don't think so!*

SERVES 6–8

*½ cup extra-virgin olive oil*
*3 large garlic cloves, crushed*
*1kg (3 medium) eggplants, thinly sliced*
*2 anchovy fillets, finely chopped* ✿
*1 brown onion, finely chopped*
*1 carrot, peeled, finely chopped*
*1 celery stick, trimmed, finely chopped*
*2 x 400g cans whole cherry tomatoes*
*2 red capsicum, roasted (see recipe page 20, step 1)*
*1 cup soft white breadcrumbs*
*60g parmesan, finely grated*
*1 cup flat-leaf parsley, chopped*
*100g bocconcini, torn in half*
*extra-virgin olive oil, to serve*

1 Preheat a barbecue grill or plate on medium heat. Combine oil and garlic in a jug and use 100ml to brush both sides of the eggplant. Barbecue the eggplant in batches for 4–5 minutes each side or until golden and tender. Set aside on a plate.

2 Heat the remaining tablespoon of garlic oil in a medium saucepan over medium-low heat. Add the anchovy and cook, stirring, for 3 minutes until the anchovy has dissolved. Add the onion, carrot and celery and cook, stirring occasionally, for 5 minutes or until soft. Add the tomatoes and bring to the boil. Reduce the heat to low and simmer uncovered for 10–15 minutes until sauce is thick. Taste and season with salt and pepper.

3 Preheat the oven to 180°C fan-forced/200°C no fan. Grease a 6cm-deep, 6-cup capacity baking dish. Roughly chop the roasted capsicum and set aside. Combine the breadcrumbs, parmesan and parsley in a bowl.

4 To assemble, spoon one-third of the sauce over the base of the baking dish. Top with half the eggplant, then half the capsicum and sprinkle with half the breadcrumb mixture. Spoon over half the remaining tomato sauce, then top with all the bocconcini. Top with the remaining eggplant and capsicum. Spoon over half the remaining breadcrumbs then all the remaining tomato sauce. Scatter the remaining crumbs over the top, drizzle with a little oil. Place onto a tray and bake, uncovered, for 25–30 minutes until bubbling around the edges.

✿ Even if you're not an anchovy fan, they are a must in this recipe. The anchovy dissolves in the oil, adding a saltiness that balances all the flavours.

# ROAST PUMPKIN & SWEET ONION TART

*This tart is great for lunch, dinner, picnics or when you're asked to take a plate. This is a version of a recipe I created recently for Jamie Durie's* The Outdoor Room *magazine.*

SERVES 4

*700g butternut pumpkin, peeled, cut into 3cm pieces*
*12 French eschalots, peeled, halved*
*4 sprigs thyme*
*2 tablespoons maple syrup*
*3 tablespoons extra-virgin olive oil*
*100g wedge fresh ricotta*
*1 egg yolk*
*30g wild rocket*
*2 teaspoons balsamic vinegar*
*pecorino, finely grated to serve*

PECORINO PASTRY

*1½ cups plain flour*
*30g (½ cup) pecorino, finely grated*
*125g butter, chilled, cubed*
*¼ cup chilled water*

1 Preheat the oven to 220°C fan-forced/230°C no fan. Combine the pumpkin, eschalots and thyme in a lightly greased roasting pan. Whisk maple syrup, 1 tablespoon of the oil, and salt and pepper in a jug, then pour over the pumpkin mixture. Toss gently to coat. Roast for 20 minutes until pumpkin and eschalots are just tender. Set aside to cool 15 minutes.

2 To make the pecorino pastry, combine the flour, pecorino and butter in a food processor. Process until mixture resembles fine breadcrumbs. Add chilled water and process until the pastry comes together. Turn onto a lightly floured surface and knead lightly until smooth. Shape into a rectangle. If it's a warm day, wrap in greaseproof paper and refrigerate for 15 minutes or until firm enough to roll out.

3 Reduce the oven temperature to 200°C fan-forced/210°C no fan and place a large flat baking tray into oven to preheat. Roll the pastry out on a large sheet of baking paper to a 16cm x 34cm rectangle.

4 Beat the ricotta and egg yolk together until creamy, then spread over the pastry, leaving a 1½ cm border around all four edges. Spoon the pumpkin and eschalots evenly over the ricotta mixture. Fold the pastry border over the pumpkin, leaving three-quarters exposed. Brush the top of the pastry with cold tap water.

5 Slide the tart (still on the baking paper) onto the hot tray and bake for 30 minutes or until pastry is golden and crisp. Toss the rocket with the balsamic and remaining oil, then scatter over the tart. Grate over plenty of pecorino, season with salt and freshly ground black pepper and serve.

# FIG, PEAR AND FENNEL SALAD

*I am a fresh fig fan, so playing around with combinations or ways to serve them is something I love to do. This one got the big tick. When fresh figs are not available, soften dried figs in boiling water as a substitute.*

SERVES 4 AS SIDE

*1 fennel bulb, trimmed*
*2 firm ripe pears*
*8 radishes, scrubbed*
*6 ripe figs, torn in half*
*½ cup feta-stuffed green olives, halved*
*100g mixed baby salad leaves*
*½ cup hazelnuts, roasted, coarsely chopped*

DRESSING

*1 ruby red grapefruit, juiced*
*2 teaspoons honey*
*⅓ cup extra-virgin olive oil*
*1 teaspoon seeded mustard*

1 For the dressing, combine all the ingredients in a screw-top jar with salt and freshly ground black pepper. Shake until well combined.

2 Thinly slice or shave the fennel, pears and radishes using a sharp knife or mandolin, then place into a large bowl. Pour over the dressing and toss to coat.

3 Add the figs, olives and salad leaves and toss gently to combine. Transfer to a serving platter, scatter over the hazelnuts and serve.

Serve salad with a thick wedge of baked ricotta and crusty bread or toss through cooked chicken and it quickly becomes dinner.

# AUTUMN SWEET

# HONEYCOMB PAVLOVAS

*Here is my take on the famous pavlova. Individually, they're so beautiful and easy to serve. If you like, you can make one large 20cm pav – it takes the same cooking time.*

MAKES 8

*4 free-range egg whites, at room temperature* ♥
*a pinch cream of tartar*
*1 cup caster sugar*
*1 tablespoon cocoa powder*
*75g chocolate-coated honeycomb, chopped*
*300ml double cream*
*cocoa powder, to serve*

LIQUEUR FUDGE SAUCE

*200g good-quality dark chocolate, chopped (Plaistowe brand)*
*1/3 cup thickened cream*
*2 tablespoons Kahlúa*

1 Preheat the oven to 120°C fan-forced/120°C no fan. Draw four 7cm circles on a piece of baking paper. Repeat with a second sheet of paper and use to line 2 large lightly greased flat baking trays, pencil marks facing down.

2 Using an electric mixer, whisk the egg whites and cream of tartar on high speed until soft peaks form. Reduce the speed to medium-low. Add sugar, 1 tablespoon at a time, beating constantly, until all the sugar is combined. After adding the final spoonful of sugar, increase the mixer speed to high and beat for 2 minutes or until meringue is thick and glossy and sugar has dissolved. Sift the cocoa powder over the meringue, add the honeycomb and gently swirl together.

3 Spoon about 1/4 cup meringue mixture per pavlova onto each circle, allowing room for spreading. Place the trays in the oven, reduce the heat to 110°C fan-forced/100°C no fan and bake for 1 1/4–1 1/2 hours or until dry to touch. Turn the oven off and open the door about 2–3cm. Allow the pavlovas to cool completely in the oven.

4 For the liqueur fudge sauce, combine chocolate and cream in a heat-proof, microwave-safe bowl. Microwave, uncovered, for 2–3 minutes on High/100%, stirring every minute with a metal spoon until smooth. Stir in the liqueur.

5 To serve, top each pavlova with cream, spoon over the warm fudge sauce and serve dusted with a little extra cocoa powder if desired.

♥ *One of the secrets to good pavlova/meringues is stable egg whites. Using egg whites that have been frozen then thawed stabilises them. One egg white is equal to 30ml, so stop throwing away those unused whites! Freeze them in a container to make this sensational dessert.*

# ANZAC BISCUITS

*Chewy or crispy – that's the debate when it comes to Anzac biscuits. The size of the biscuits and the cooking time is the difference. What matters at the end of the day is making these biscuits with kids and remembering our Anzac heroes, while embracing the freedom and extraordinary life we live.*

MAKES 36 SMALL OR 24 REGULAR

*1 cup plain flour*
*1 cup rolled oats* ✿
*¾ cup caster sugar*
*¾ cup desiccated coconut*
*150g butter, cubed, chopped*
*1 tablespoon golden syrup*
*1 tablespoon cold tap water*
*1 teaspoon bicarbonate of soda*

✿ For best results use the original oats, not the instant ones.

1 Preheat the oven to 160°C fan-forced/170°C no fan. Line 3 large baking trays with baking paper.

2 Sift the flour into a large bowl. Add the rolled oats, sugar and coconut and stir to combine.

3 Melt the butter and golden syrup in a small saucepan over medium heat until hot. Combine the cold water and bicarbonate of soda, then add to the hot butter and stir to combine. (It will bubble.) Pour the hot butter mixture quickly into the flour and stir until well combined.

4 Roll heaped teaspoons of mixture into balls and place onto trays, allowing plenty of room for spreading. Use a spatula to flatten slightly. Bake two trays at a time, swapping trays around halfway through, for 12 minutes for chewy Anzac biscuits or 15 minutes for crunchy ones. Stand biscuits on the trays for 5 minutes, then transfer to wire racks to cool.

VARIATIONS:

*Sultana Anzacs:* add ¼ cup sultanas to the mixture with the butter in step 3.

*Macadamia Anzacs:* add ½ cup toasted chopped macadamia nuts to the mixture and reduce the coconut to ½ cup in step 2 with oats.

# PLUM & OAT COBBLER

*As the weather turns a little cooler and all the stone fruit disappears, this is a great way to enjoy the last of the plums. Once they've gone, use canned fruit or roasted apple and rhubarb for another fabulous combination.*

SERVES 4

*8 large firm ripe plums, halved* ✿
*2 tablespoons fruit juice (like cranberry, pomegranate or apple)*
*2 tablespoons white sugar*
*1 cup self-raising flour*
*¼ cup cornmeal (polenta)*
*¼ cup caster sugar*
*100g butter, chilled, chopped*
*⅓ cup rolled oats*
*½ cup buttermilk*
*¼ cup flaked almonds*
*vanilla ice-cream, to serve*

✿ Mariposa, blood plums or sugar plums make the best cobbler.

1 Preheat the oven to 200°C fan-forced/220°C no fan. Remove the stones from the plums. Arrange the plums cut side up in a 4cm-deep, 22cm (base) (about 5-cup capacity) baking dish so the fruit fits snugly. Pour over the fruit juice, then sprinkle with 1 tablespoon of the white sugar. ♥

2 Combine the flour, cornmeal, caster sugar and butter in a food processor and process until the mixture resembles fine breadcrumbs. Transfer the mixture to a bowl. Stir in the oats. Make a well in the centre and pour in the buttermilk. Stir with a table knife to form a soft dough, adding more buttermilk if required.

3 Drop spoonfuls of dough over the fruit, leaving some fruit exposed. Sprinkle with almonds then the remaining 1 tablespoon of white sugar. Bake for 25–30 minutes until the top is golden. Serve warm with ice-cream.

♥ The white sugar prevents the fruit from collapsing completely.

# VANILLA-GLAZED YOGHURT CAKE

*You know the delicious glazed doughnuts that have popped up all over the world? (If not, that's good.) Well, this glaze is as close as you will get. It's sweet, vanilla-y and perfect over my yoghurt cake.*

SERVES 8

*150g butter, cubed, softened*
*1 cup caster sugar*
*1 teaspoon vanilla bean paste*
*2 x 59g eggs, at room temperature* ✿
*1½ cups self-raising flour, sifted*
*150ml Greek-style yoghurt*

VANILLA GLAZE

*½ cup icing sugar mixture, sifted*
*20g butter, melted*
*1 tablespoon boiling water*
*1 teaspoon vanilla bean paste*

1 Preheat the oven to 160°C fan-forced/170°C no fan. Grease and line base and sides of a round 20cm (base) cake pan. ♥

2 Using an electric mixer, ♦ beat the butter, caster sugar and vanilla until pale and creamy, scraping down the sides of the bowl occasionally. Add the eggs one at a time, beating until just combined. (Over-beating will cause the cake batter to curdle.)

3 Fold in the flour followed by the yoghurt until just combined. Spoon the mixture into the pan and smooth the surface – this helps the cake rise evenly. Bake for 45–50 minutes or until a skewer inserted into the centre comes out clean. Let the cake stand in the pan for 5 minutes before turning onto a wire rack.

4 For the vanilla glaze, combine all the ingredients in a bowl and mix until smooth. Spoon the warm glaze over the warm cake and set aside to cool or enjoy warm.

✿ It is important to have both the butter and eggs at room temperature. If they are cold, the mixture will curdle when the eggs are added, giving the cake a heavy, coarse and uneven texture.

♥ This cake can also be cooked in a square 18cm (base) cake pan. The cooking time is the same.

♦ It is best to use the flat or K beater, not the whisk attachment.

# MASCARPONE FIG TART

SERVES 8

*½ cup flaked almonds*
*1 tablespoon maple syrup*
*2 tablespoons icing sugar*
*6 medium fresh figs, halved*
*2 tablespoons white sugar*
*2 eggs*
*2 teaspoons vanilla bean paste*
*3 tablespoons caster sugar*
*1 tablespoon cornflour*
*200ml thickened cream*
*250g mascarpone cream cheese*

PASTRY

*1½ cups plain flour*
*⅓ cup pure icing sugar*
*125g butter, chilled, cubed*
*2 egg yolks*
*2–3 tablespoons chilled water*

♥ If you are using rice, allow it to cool completely then store in an airtight container and re-use for blind-baking.

1 For the pastry, combine the flour, icing sugar and butter in a food processor. Process until mixture resembles breadcrumbs. Add the egg yolks and 2 tablespoons of water. Process until the pastry comes together, adding the remaining water if necessary. Turn onto a lightly floured surface and knead gently until smooth. Press the pastry into a 15cm round and wrap in greaseproof paper. (Don't use plastic as this causes pastry to sweat.) Refrigerate for 15 minutes until firm enough to roll out.

2 Roll the pastry between 2 large sheets of baking paper to a 32cm round. Use the pastry to line the base and sides of a 2.5cm-deep, 26cm (base) loose-based flan. Trim the edges. Refrigerate for 30 minutes. Preheat the oven and a large flat tray to 180°C fan-forced/200°C no fan.

3 Combine the almonds, maple syrup and icing sugar in a bowl. Spread onto a sheet of baking paper, then place onto the hot tray in the oven. Bake for 5–10 minutes or until golden. Carefully lift the almonds and baking paper onto a wire rack, then set aside to cool. Return tray to the oven.

4 Press the cut side of the figs into the white sugar. Heat a large frying pan over high heat until hot. Place a sheet of baking paper into the hot pan, then place 4 fig halves, sugar side down, into the pan. Cook for 1 minute or until golden. Remove to a plate and repeat twice with remaining figs.

5 Pierce the pastry base with a fork. Scrunch up and then flatten out a large piece of greaseproof paper and use to line the base and sides of the flan. Half fill the flan with baking beans or raw rice. Place the tart onto the hot tray, and bake for 15 minutes until the pastry edges are light golden. Remove the beans and paper, ♥ return the tart to the oven and bake 8–10 minutes until light golden all over. Remove from the oven. Reduce the oven to 160°C fan-forced/170°C no fan.

6 Arrange the sugared figs over the base of the tart. Using a fork, beat eggs, vanilla, sugar and cornflour until combined. (You don't want bubbles in the mixture.) Gently stir in the cream then mascarpone and pour over the figs. Return to the oven and bake 35–40 minutes or until set in the centre. Break up the almonds and scatter over the tart. Serve warm or cold.

# TRIPLE-CHOCOLATE PANNA COTTA MOUSSE

*Some days, testing in the kitchen creates something new and wonderful. This recipe came about when I was testing two recipes that were pretty good on their own, but combined . . . as the kids of today say, 'OMG!'*

MAKES 6

MILK CHOCOLATE MOUSSE

*200g quality milk chocolate*
*60ml Kahlúa*
*2 free-range eggs, separated*
*1 tablespoon caster sugar*
*150ml thickened cream*
*Turkish delight skewers to serve, optional*

DARK CHOCOLATE FUDGE

*100g quality dark chocolate, chopped*
*2 tablespoons brewed espresso coffee*

WHITE CHOCOLATE PANNA COTTA

*1 cup thickened cream*
*1 teaspoon vanilla bean paste*
*¼ cup caster sugar*
*1 tablespoon cold water*
*1 teaspoon gelatine powder*
*60g quality white chocolate, coarsely chopped*
*1 cup Greek-style yoghurt*

1 For the milk chocolate mousse, melt the milk chocolate in a clean, dry, large, heat-proof microwave-safe bowl in 1 minute bursts on Medium/50%, stirring every minute with a metal spoon until smooth. Microwave the Kahlúa for 20 seconds on High/100% until warm, then stir into the warm chocolate with the egg yolks.

2 Beat the egg whites with an electric hand mixer to soft peaks. Add the sugar and beat until well combined. Stir one-third into the chocolate mixture, then carefully fold the remaining egg whites into the chocolate mousse until just combined.

3 Whip the cream to soft peaks then fold into the chocolate mousse. Spoon the mousse into six 1-cup capacity glasses. Cover and refrigerate for 2 hours until set.

4 For the dark chocolate fudge, combine the chocolate and espresso in a microwave-safe bowl. Microwave, uncovered, in 30-second bursts on High/100%, stirring with a metal spoon until melted and smooth. Cool for 10 minutes, then carefully spoon a thin layer over the milk chocolate mousse. Refrigerate for 30 minutes to set.

5 For the white chocolate panna cotta, combine the cream, vanilla and sugar in a small saucepan. Combine the cold water and gelatine in a bowl, then add to the cream mixture. Place the pan over medium heat for 4–5 minutes or until the mixture is hot, stirring constantly to dissolve the sugar and gelatine.

6 Place white chocolate in a large bowl, pour over the hot cream mixture and stir until smooth. Stir in the yoghurt, then set aside to cool for 30 minutes. Strain the mixture into a jug then pour about ¼ cup into each glass. Cover and refrigerate 6 hours or overnight if time allows. Serve with Turkish delight if desired.

# HONEY-ROASTED APPLES AND PEARS

*This is a delicious midweek dessert and great way to add more fresh fruit to your daily diet. If the ricotta is really fresh and whipped until smooth, it tastes just like cream!*

SERVES 4

*2 vanilla beans, split* ✿
*50g butter, chopped*
*¼ cup honey*
*3 Golden Delicious apples*
*3 Beurre Bosc pears*

RICOTTA CREAM

*125g wedge fresh ricotta*
*2 tablespoons honey*
*2 teaspoons vanilla bean paste*

1 Preheat the oven and a large roasting pan to 220°C fan-forced/240°C no fan.

2 Scrape the seeds from the vanilla beans with a teaspoon. Combine the butter, honey, vanilla seeds and beans in a small saucepan over medium heat. Heat for 3–4 minutes until the butter is hot. Remove from the heat.

3 Cut the apples and pears into quarters and remove the core and seeds. Remove the hot tray from the oven, place a sheet of baking paper over the base, then add the apples and pears. Remove the vanilla beans from the pan, then pour the warm butter mixture over the fruit and toss to coat.

4 Roast for 15–20 minutes, turning the fruit after 10 minutes, or until golden and only just tender.

5 For the ricotta cream, combine the ricotta, honey and vanilla in a bowl. Using an electric hand mixer, beat the ricotta until light and creamy. Serve with the warm fruit and pan juices.

✿ If you don't have vanilla beans, just use a little vanilla bean paste or extract.

# CHOCOLATE WEET-BIX SLICE

*Everyone needs a quick, one-bowl, go-to slice that can be thrown together – here's mine.*

MAKES 16 PIECES

*125g butter, chopped*
*3 tablespoons cocoa powder*
*1 cup brown sugar*
*1 egg, lightly beaten*
*½ teaspoon vanilla extract*
*1 cup self-raising flour*
*½ cup desiccated coconut*
*4 Weet-Bix cereal biscuits, crushed* ♥

CHOCOLATE ICING

*200g quality dark or milk chocolate, chopped (Plaistowe brand)*
*⅓ cup sour cream, at room temperature*

1 Preheat the oven to 170°C fan-forced/180°C no fan. Grease and line the base and sides of a 20cm (base) square cake pan with baking paper.

2 Place the butter in a large heat-proof, microwave-safe (such as Pyrex) bowl and microwave, uncovered, for 1–2 minutes on Medium/50% until melted and warm. Add the cocoa powder and stir until dissolved. Stir in the remaining ingredients and mix well.

3 Using a large metal spoon, press the mixture into the base of the cake pan. Bake for 18–20 minutes or until a skewer inserted into the centre comes out clean. Set aside to cool.

4 For the chocolate icing, microwave the chocolate in a medium heat-proof, microwave-safe bowl, uncovered, for 2–3 minutes on Medium/50%, stirring every minute with a metal spoon until melted. Stir in the sour cream, then spread over the cool slice. Allow to set before cutting into pieces.

♥ Four crushed Weet-Bix will give you 1 cup crushed cereal. (We often have crushed Weet-Bix in the bottom of the box, so this recipe is a perfect way to use them up.)

# CREAMY, SALTY PEANUT CARAMELS

*As an 8- or 9-year-old, I used to make this with two girlfriends. At that stage I wasn't much of a cook and we never followed the recipe, so from time to time it didn't set. That never mattered – we would sit around our family swimming pool, legs dangling in the water, eating the soft caramel with a spoon. Any leftovers were swirled through vanilla ice-cream!*

MAKES 40

*395g can sweetened condensed milk*
*2 tablespoons golden syrup*
*2 tablespoons glucose syrup* ♥
*50g butter, chopped*
*2 teaspoons vanilla bean paste*
*½ cup peanut butter*
*1 cup salted peanuts*
*200g quality dark or white chocolate, melted, optional*

1 Grease and line base and side of an 8cm x 30cm (base) loaf pan with baking paper.

2 Combine the condensed milk, golden syrup, glucose and butter in an 8-cup capacity heatproof, microwave-safe Pyrex bowl. Microwave, uncovered, for 3 minutes on High/100%, whisking every minute with a balloon whisk. Then microwave a further 4 minutes, stopping and whisking every 30 seconds, or until the caramel is light golden and thickened.

3 Quickly add the vanilla, peanut butter and peanuts and stir until combined. Spoon the hot caramel into the loaf pan, smooth the surface and set aside on a wire rack to cool. Cover and refrigerate overnight.

4 Cut into pieces, dip in melted chocolate if desired and refrigerate until set, then wrap in wax paper and store in an airtight jar in the fridge.

♥ Glucose syrup is also known as liquid glucose. It's available from some supermarkets in the baking aisle near the sugar, or health food stores. It prevents the caramel from crystallising.

# WINTER

*Cool crisp days, weekend sleep-ins, lazy Sunday afternoons at the football, the house filled with aromas of sweet baking and simmering casseroles – this is what I look forward to in winter.*

# BEST BUYS

## FRUIT

### JUNE

*apples:*
- *Fuji, Red Delicious, Pink Lady, Gala, Granny Smith, Jazz*

*bananas*
*custard apples*
*fresh dates*
*lemons*
*mandarins:*
- *Imperial*

*nashi pears*
*oranges:*
- *naval*

*passionfruit*
*pears:*
- *Beurre Bosc, Packham, Corella*

*quince*
*rhubarb*
*tangelos*

### JULY

*apples:*
- *Golden and Red Delicious, Granny Smith, Pink Lady, Fuji*

*bananas*
*berries:*
- *strawberries*

*custard apples*
*dates*
*grapefuit:*
- *ruby red*

*lemons*
*mandarins:*
- *Imperial, Ellendale*

*nashi pears*
*oranges:*
- *Seville*

*pears:*
- *Beurre Bosc, Packham, Corella*

*rhubarb*
*tamarillos*
*tangelos*

### AUGUST

*bananas*
*berries:*
- *strawberries*

*custard apples*
*dates*
*grapefuit:*
- *ruby red*

*lemons*
*mandarins:*
- *Ellendale*

*nashi pears*
*oranges:*
- *blood*

*pears:*
- *Beurre Bosc, Packham, Corella*

*rhubarb*
*strawberries*
*tamarillos*
*tangelos*

# VEGETABLES

## JUNE

- *Asian greens:*
  - *choy sum*
- *avocados:*
  - *Sharwil, Hass*
- *beans:*
  - *green*
- *beetroot*
- *broccoli*
- *brussels sprouts*
- *cabbage:*
  - *green*
- *carrots*
- *cauliflower*
- *celery*
- *chillies*
- *fennel*
- *garlic*
- *ginger*
- *leeks*
- *mushrooms*
- *onions*
- *parsnips*
- *peas:*
  - *sugar snap*
- *potatoes*
- *pumpkin*
- *silverbeet and English spinach*
- *squash and zucchini*
- *swedes*
- *sweet potato*
- *turnips*

## JULY

- *artichoke:*
  - *Jerusalem*
- *avocados:*
  - *Sharwil, Hass*
- *beans:*
  - *green*
- *beetroot*
- *broccoli*
- *brussels sprouts*
- *cabbage:*
  - *green*
- *carrots:*
  - *baby*
- *cauliflower*
- *celery*
- *chillies*
- *fennel*
- *garlic*
- *ginger*
- *leek*
- *mushrooms*
- *onions*
- *parsnips*
- *peas:*
  - *sugar snap and green*
- *potatoes*
- *pumpkin:*
  - *butternut*
- *radishes*
- *silverbeet and English spinach*
- *swedes*
- *sweet potato*
- *turnips*
- *zucchini*

## AUGUST

- *artichoke:*
  - *Globe*
- *asparagus*
- *avocados:*
  - *Hass*
- *beans:*
  - *green*
- *beetroot*
- *broccoli*
- *brussels sprouts*
- *cabbage:*
  - *green*
- *carrots:*
  - *baby*
- *cauliflower*
- *celery*
- *chillies*
- *fennel:*
  - *baby*
- *garlic*
- *ginger*
- *leek*
- *mushrooms*
- *onions*
- *parsnips*
- *peas:*
  - *snow and green*
- *potatoes*
- *pumpkin:*
  - *butternut*
- *radishes*
- *silverbeet and English spinach*
- *swedes*
- *sweet potato*
- *turnips*
- *zucchini*

# PRODUCE

## PEARS

They're up there with mangoes when it comes to my favourite fruit. The natural sugar content (fructose), varies considerably in each variety, which is why some pears are suitable for cooking, some for eating and others for salads.

Packham has pale-green skin that changes to yellow as it ripens. The juicy flesh is smooth and sweet. Perfect eaten raw or cooked. The flesh will hold its shape when cooked.

Beurre Bosc has a long, slender neck with a cinnamon-brown skin. Its firm, dry flesh is my preferred cooking pear for both sweet and savoury. It, too, holds it shape and texture without releasing too much moisture, making it perfect for baking.

Williams are medium to large in size and have yellow-green skin. They are slow to ripen. Once ripe, they have soft, white, juicy flesh. Great poached, juiced or used raw in salads.

Red Sensation has a stunning crimson-red skin that intensifies in colour as it ripens. It's sweet but not overly juicy. Suitable for both eating and great in salads.

Corella is a small pear with green speckled skin with crimson-red and gold streaks. Corella can be eaten raw, firm or soft, and is great for poaching.

Nashi is not a cross between apple and pear as many think – it is a unique Asian species. Unlike other pears, it does not brown when cut and is picked ripe. It has a sweet, juicy, crisp (apple-like) flesh and thin, yellow-green skin. Use raw in salads, on cheese plates or eat fresh.

I tasted Ya Li pears in Shepparton this year for the first time. They are delicious, so keep an eye out for them. Ya Li is a pear-shaped Nashi with greenish-yellow skin. Best enjoyed raw, icy cold from the fridge.

*Storage:* Unripe pears should be stored in a single layer in a basket at room temperature, out of direct sunlight. Once ripe, store in a single layer in an open plastic bag (starved of oxygen, pears will start to rot quickly from the core) on the lowest shelf in the fridge for up to 3 days.

*Best buddies with*: Butter, cream and ice-cream; blue cheese, parmesan and soft white cheese; walnuts, pistachio and pecans; vanilla, cinnamon and ginger; pork, ham and duck; berries and spinach and rocket.

## LEMONS

One of the most versatile ingredients in the kitchen. Used for sweet and savoury, they're rated as invaluable to almost every cuisine.

Lisbon is a commonly grown, backyard lemon. With a shiny, bright-yellow, thin, smooth skin, they have a thick pith, plenty of juice, minimal seeds and are quite tart – perfect for home-made cordial.

Meyer is a cross between a lemon and an orange, so they're sweeter than other varieties. They have a smooth yellowy-orange skin and are perfect for salads and dressings.

Eureka have a prominent point at one end and slightly bumpy skin. Medium-thin skinned, they contain plenty of juice. They are quite bitter, contain seeds high in pectin, and are perfect for jam-making.

*Tip*: Microwave uncut, room-temperature lemons for 15 seconds on High/100% or roll them on the bench to release as much as double the juice before cutting and squeezing.

*Tip*: Rub cut side of lemon over warm barbecue to remove baked-on food.

*Best buddies with*: Chicken, lamb, veal and fish; cream and eggs; noodles, rice and pasta; fresh berries; dried and fresh chilli; lentils and chickpeas; honey, sugar – white, brown and palm.

## RHUBARB

There is no substitute for the rose-pink colour and sweet-sour taste rhubarb creates when cooked. Roasted, stewed or baked, it makes the best pies, crumbles and jam.

*Storage*: Rhubarb perishes quickly at room temperature, so store – unwashed, uncut – in a plastic bag in the fridge crisper. Cooked rhubarb will keep 5-7 days in a clean Pyrex (not plastic) container.

*Preparation*: Always remove and discard the leaves as they are poisonous. Trim the base and wash each stalk well. Some rhubarb contains 'strings' similar to celery – these should be removed.

*Best buddies with*: Apples, pears plums, cherries and strawberries; honey and sugar; vanilla, rosewater and cinnamon; butter, yoghurt, custard and ice-cream; hazelnuts and almonds; soft white cheese; pork; oats.

## POTATOES

Remember when the choice we had was dirty or washed? Now spoilt for choice, buying the right potato for the right use is a minefield.

*Best all-rounders*: Sebago, Golden Delight. Great for chips, roasting, boiling, baking and mash.

*Best chips*: Russet Burbank, Bintje, Coliban or Spunta.
*Tip*: Use peanut oil for frying and drain on a wire rack, not paper towel.

*Best mash*: Desiree, Sebago, Coliban, Pontiac or Spunta.
*Tip*: After boiling, drain well and return to hot pan and shake dry. Always use hot milk to mash.

*Best salad*: Kipfler, Nicola or Pink-eye.
*Tip*: Bring to boil in cold water. Once cooked, pour half the dressing over the hot potatoes and allow them to soak up dressing. With Kipfler and other thin-skinned potatoes, boil or steam without peeling.

*Best roast*: Sebago, Chats, Golden Delight or King Edward.
*Tip*: Parboil then drain well. Return to hot pan and shake dry, roughing up surface. Add hot potatoes to hot oil in the roasting pan.

*Best jacket-baked*: Pontiac or Sebago.
*Tip*: Always pierce potatoes and don't wrap in foil to cook.

*Best smashed*: Coliban, Chats or Cream Delight.
*Tip*: Parboil, steam or microwave potatoes until tender. Squash while hot, then drizzle with oil and roast towards top of the oven.

*Best hash browns*: Sebago and Golden Delight.
*Tip*: Grate the potatoes into a clean tea towel and squeeze as much moisture from the potato as you can.

*Storage*: Keep in a well-ventilated, dark cupboard, either in a basket or brown paper bag. Do not store in plastic bags as this causes them to sweat and deteriorate quickly.

*Best buddies with*: Butter and olive oil; milk, cream and stock; onions, garlic and leeks; cumin, coriander and saffron; bay leaves, rosemary, sage and parsley; mozzarella, Swiss and fontina cheese.

## PUMPKIN

Highly prized in the Mediterranean, Middle East and Australia, it's one of the vegetables on almost everyone's weekly shopping list.

Queensland Blue: Has a blue-grey, smooth, deeply ribbed skin. Its golden-orange flesh is full-flavoured. Best steamed or microwaved, then puréed. Famously used for scones.

Butternut: The most versatile of all. Pear-shaped with a dense, dry, sweet-tasting flesh. Great for roasting, mashing and soups.

Jarrahdale: Closely resembles the Queensland Blue, but is grey and not as deeply ribbed. Its thinner skin makes it easier to cut and peel.

Japanese or Kent: Its green-grey skin is mottled with yellow and brown. Its dry flesh has a rich, nutty taste and is great for roasting.

*Tip*: Remove the seeds and membrane from cut pumpkin before tightly covering in plastic wrap and storing in the fridge, as the seeds and membrane are the first to go mouldy, causing the flesh to deteriorate quickly.

*Best buddies with*: Sage, thyme and rosemary; vanilla, allspice, cinnamon, nutmeg, cloves and ginger; apples and oranges; almonds and walnuts; cured meats; blue cheese, goats' curd, mozzarella, ricotta; chickpeas, coconut milk, cream, crème fraîche; honey and maple syrup; lamb, pork, prawns.

# WINTER SAVOURY

# SPINACH SOUP

*During winter, this soup (along with my creamy pumpkin) is my go-to soup. I like to add bacon, chicken and fresh herbs. It's quick, easy, delicious, filling and good for you.*

SERVES 4

*2 tablespoons olive oil*
*2 brown onions, halved, thinly sliced*
*1 garlic clove, crushed*
*¼ (about 250g) cauliflower, trimmed, chopped* ✿
*4–5 cups chicken or vegetable stock*
*30g butter*
*2 bunches English spinach leaves, washed, shredded*
*¼ teaspoon freshly grated nutmeg*
*1 lemon, rind finely grated, juiced*
*4 tablespoons thickened cream, optional*
*toasted sourdough, to serve*

1 Heat the olive oil in a large saucepan over a medium-low heat. Add the onions and garlic and cook slowly, stirring occasionally for 10 minutes or until soft (but not coloured). Add the cauliflower and cook a further 5 minutes or until it starts to soften.

2 Pour in 4 cups of the stock, increase the heat to medium and simmer gently, uncovered, for about 10 minutes or until the cauliflower is nice and tender.

3 Meanwhile, melt the butter in a deep large frying pan over medium heat. Add spinach and sauté for 2–3 minutes or until it just starts to wilt. Add the nutmeg and lemon rind and toss to combine. Add the sautéed spinach to the cauliflower mixture, remove from the heat and allow to cool a little before blending.

4 Blend or puree the soup in batches until smooth. Return to the saucepan. Add 2 tablespoons of the lemon juice and season to taste with salt and freshly ground black pepper. Bring the soup back to a simmer, adding more stock if required at this stage to reach the consistency you desire. Swirl through the cream if using and serve with toasted sourdough.

✿ You can replace the cauliflower with 3 medium sebago potatoes, peeled and chopped, or a 400g can drained and well-rinsed cannellini beans.

# HAM, CHEESE & MUSTARD SCHIACCIATA

*A schiacciata is an Italian flatbread made famous in Tuscany. Surprisingly, I experienced this dish in Hawaii!*

SERVES 4

*2 tablespoons olive oil*
*1 large brown onion, very finely chopped*
*2 garlic cloves, crushed*
*2 tablespoons Dijon or hot mustard*
*300g piece leg ham, finely chopped*
*125g semi-dried tomatoes, chopped*
*175g cheddar, coarsely grated*
*125g wedge fresh ricotta*
*baby rocket leaves, dressed, to serve*

YEAST DOUGH

*¾ cup lukewarm water*
*7g instant dried yeast*
*½ teaspoon caster sugar*
*1 teaspoon sea salt flakes*
*¼ cup extra-virgin olive oil*
*2⅔ cups bread flour or plain flour*

1 For the yeast dough, combine the warm water, yeast, sugar, salt and extra-virgin olive oil in a large bowl. Add the flour and stir to form a soft dough. Turn onto a lightly floured surface and knead for 8 minutes, until elastic, adding a little more flour if the dough is sticky. Place in a lightly oiled bowl, cover with plastic wrap and set aside in a warm place for 50–60 minutes or until the dough has doubled in size.

2 Meanwhile, heat half the olive oil in a small non-stick frying pan over medium heat. Add onion and garlic and cook, stirring, for 5–8 minutes or until soft. Set aside to cool.

Knock down the dough and divide in half. Press or roll one half out to a 26cm round on a sheet of baking paper. Spread the mustard right to the edge, then top with the onions. Sprinkle over the ham, tomatoes and cheddar, then crumble over the ricotta.

4 Press or roll the remaining dough to a 26cm round and place over the ham and cheese mixture. Press the edges together to seal. Cover loosely and set aside in a warm place for 20 minutes.

5 Preheat the oven and a large flat tray to 200°C fan-forced/220°C no fan. Using your fingertips, press randomly into the top of the dough, leaving dimples. Drizzle the schiacciata with the remaining olive oil and season with salt and freshly ground black pepper. Bake on the hot tray for 30–35 minutes or until golden. Cut into 8 wedges, scatter over rocket leaves and serve.

VARIATION

For spinach and feta schiacciata, replace the ham with shredded English spinach and the cheddar with feta and omit the mustard.

# ROAST BEETROOT SALAD

*I confess that I love canned baby beets, but when fresh beetroot is on the shelf you can't really compare the two.*

SERVES 4 AS SIDE

*1 bunch medium (about 700g) beetroot, peeled*
*1 bunch baby carrots, scrubbed*
*1/3 cup extra-virgin olive oil*
*2 teaspoons brown sugar*
*1 teaspoon horseradish cream*
*½ orange, juiced*
*2 oranges, peeled, segmented*
*½ cup walnuts, toasted, coarsely chopped*
*100g salad leaves* ♥
*50g goats' cheese*

1 Preheat the oven to 180°C fan-forced/200°C no fan. Remove the leaves from the beetroot and set any small leaves aside. Trim the roots and stems of the beets, leaving about 2cm of each stem. Cut into quarters or eighths depending on their size. Place in a large greased roasting pan and add the carrots.

2 Combine the olive oil, brown sugar, horseradish cream, 2 tablespoons orange juice and salt and pepper in a screw-top jar and shake well to combine. Pour half the dressing over the beetroot and carrots and toss to coat. Roast for 30–40 minutes or until the vegetables are tender. Set aside to cool for 15 minutes.

3 Add the orange segments, walnuts, salad leaves and any reserved beetroot leaves to the pan. Crumble over the goats' cheese and pour over remaining dressing. Toss gently to combine. Pile onto a platter and serve with crispy roast pork belly (see recipe page 166).

♥ It depends on the beetroot you buy, but there may be enough beautiful fresh leaves on the bunch that can be added to the salad. If not, 100g of baby beetroot leaves, rocket or mixed leaves will work.

# RICOTTA BAKED PASTA SHELLS WITH BASIL PESTO

*Tomato, pasta and basil pesto is a classic any time of the year, though baked this way it's a great winter warmer the family will request every week.*

SERVES 4

*2 tablespoons olive oil*
*1 brown onion, finely chopped*
*2 large garlic cloves, crushed*
*800g can whole peeled tomatoes*
*pinch white sugar*
*1½ teaspoons dried oregano*
*400g large shell pasta* ✿
*600g wedge fresh ricotta*
*50g parmesan, finely grated*
*3 egg yolks*
*200g mozzarella, grated*

BASIL PESTO

*1½ cups firmly packed basil leaves*
*2 tablespoons pine nuts, toasted*
*½ small garlic clove, chopped*
*½ teaspoon sea salt flakes*
*¼ teaspoon freshly ground black pepper*
*150ml extra-virgin olive oil*

✿ Large pasta shapes, like the shells used here, are available from greengrocers or specialty food stores.

1 Heat the oil in a saucepan over medium heat. Add the onion and garlic and cook for 5 minutes or until the onion is soft. Add the tomatoes, sugar and a good pinch of salt and plenty of freshly ground pepper. Cook, breaking up the tomatoes with a wooden spoon, for 10 minutes or until the sauce comes to the boil.

2 Reduce the heat to medium-low and simmer, uncovered, for 10 minutes. Allow to cool for 10 minutes, then process until almost smooth. Stir in the oregano.

3 For the basil pesto, combine basil leaves, pine nuts, garlic and salt and pepper in a food processor. Pulse until finely chopped. With the motor running, gradually add the oil to form a thick paste. Transfer to a bowl and press a piece of plastic wrap right onto the surface to prevent the pesto oxidising.

4 Cook the pasta in a large saucepan of boiling salted water for half the time recommended on the packet – the pasta needs to be firm and hold its shape. Drain carefully, spread onto a greased tray and set aside to cool slightly.

5 Beat the ricotta, parmesan, egg yolks, three quarters of the mozzarella and 2 tablespoons of the pesto together until just combined. Season with salt and pepper, then use to fill the pasta shells.

6 Preheat the oven to 180°C fan-forced/200°C no fan. Spoon the tomato sauce into the base of an 8-cup capacity greased baking dish. Poke the pasta shells into the sauce. Cover tightly with foil and bake for 15 minutes. Increase the oven to 220°C fan-forced/230°C no fan, remove the foil and sprinkle over the remaining mozzarella. Bake uncovered for 8–10 minutes, or until light golden on top. Spoon over some of the remaining basil pesto and serve.

# SPANAKOPITA PIES

*These pies are oh-so delicious, whether hot out of the oven or cold for lunch, making them a pretty handy recipe to master.*

MAKES 6

*2 bunches silverbeet*
*1 tablespoon olive oil*
*2 brown onions, finely chopped*
*3 garlic cloves, crushed*
*1 lemon, rind finely grated*
*½ teaspoon ground nutmeg*
*2 tablespoons dill leaves, chopped*
*2 tablespoons flat-leaf parsley, chopped*
*4 eggs, lightly whisked*
*300g Greek feta*
*125g ghee, melted* ✿
*375g pkt filo pastry (Antoniou brand)*
*1 tablespoon sesame seeds*
*lemon wedges, to serve*

✿ Ghee, or clarified butter, has a very low water content that helps provide golden, crisp, dry filo pastry when baked. You will find it near curry pastes in the supermarket.

1 Remove leaves from the silverbeet stalks, rinse and pat them dry, then shred the leaves (not too finely). Pile half the leaves onto a large microwave-safe plate. Cover with damp paper towel and microwave for 1 minute on High/100% until the leaves just start to wilt. Transfer silverbeet to a large bowl. Repeat with remaining silverbeet.

2 Heat the oil in a small non-stick frying pan over medium heat. Add the onion and garlic and cook, stirring occasionally, for 5 minutes or until softened. Remove from heat, add the lemon rind and nutmeg. Add the onion mixture to the spinach with the dill and parsley. Add the eggs to the warm spinach mixture and mix until well combined. Crumble over the feta, season well with salt and pepper and set aside to cool.

3 Preheat the oven and a large tray to 200°C fan-forced/220°C no fan. Lightly grease six 3cm-deep, 11cm (top) pie tins with a little of the melted ghee. Lightly brush 1 filo sheet with melted ghee. Top with another sheet and brush with ghee. Cut the pastry in half crossways and use both halves to line the base and sides of 1 pie tin. Trim the excess pastry with scissors, leaving about 1cm overhang right around the tin. Repeat five times to line all pie tins. Divide the spinach filling between all pies.

4 Brush 1 filo sheet with melted ghee. Top with another sheet and brush with ghee. Fold filo in half crossways so you have four layers of filo. Place over one pie. Roll the pastry top and sides together. Brush the top of pie with ghee and sprinkle with sesame seeds. Repeat five times to finish remaining pies.

5 Use a sharp knife to cut 3 small slits in the top of each pie. Place onto the hot oven tray and bake for 25–30 minutes or until the pastry is golden. Serve warm or cold with lemon wedges.

# MY NEW APRICOT CHICKEN

*Growing up, Mum used to make us a version of this dish using a packet of French onion soup mix and we loved it. There are just too much salt and preservatives for me to continue with this family tradition. I promise this is just as good, and better for you and your family's health.*

SERVES 4

*½ cup plain flour*
*2 tablespoons Ras el Hanout or Moroccan spice blend* ✿
*1kg chicken cutlets, trimmed*
*2 tablespoons olive oil*
*1 large brown onion, halved, thinly sliced*
*3 garlic cloves, crushed*
*1½ cups apricot nectar*
*1 cup dried apricots*
*2 tablespoons flaked almonds, toasted*
*⅓ cup flat-leaf parsley, chopped*
*rice, pasta or couscous, to serve*

1 Preheat the oven to 180°C fan-forced/200°C no fan. Combine the flour and spice in a shallow dish. Coat the chicken pieces in the flour, making sure they are well coated.

2 Heat 1 tablespoon oil in a large, heavy-based frying pan over medium-high heat. Cook half the chicken for 3 minutes each side or until golden. Transfer to a baking dish. Repeat with remaining chicken and oil. Cover and set aside.

3 Drain any excess fat from the pan and add the onion and garlic, and a little more oil if needed. Cook, stirring and scraping the base to dissolve the flour bits on the base of the pan, for 3–4 minutes or until onions soften. Stir in the apricot nectar and bring to the boil. Pour the sauce over the chicken. Cover tightly with two layers of foil and bake for 30 minutes. Meanwhile, pour ½ cup boiling water over the dried apricots, cover and allow to stand.

4 Remove the foil from the chicken, add the apricots, poking them into the sauce, and cook a further 10–15 minutes, uncovered, or until the chicken is golden and cooked through. Scatter over the almonds and parsley and serve with rice, pasta or couscous.

✿ Ras el Hanout is a classic Moroccan blend of around 15-20 spices. There are many combinations available but you can't go past Herbie's blend available from www.herbies.com.au.

# CHICKEN MILANESE BURGER

*This is the fancy Italian name for a chicken schnitzel burger. Home-made is better than anything you will buy as take-away. Pile up the salad and then it's guilt-free. When serving this as a main meal to hearty eaters, double the chicken quantity below.*

MAKES 4

*2 chicken breast fillets, trimmed*
*¼ cup plain flour*
*¼ cup self-raising flour*
*1¼ cups dried breadcrumbs*
*⅓ cup finely grated parmesan cheese*
*2 eggs*
*olive oil, for cooking*
*4 soft bread rolls or hamburger buns, split*
*1 avocado, mashed*
*1 tablespoon extra-virgin olive oil*
*2 teaspoons balsamic vinegar*
*1 ripe tomato, diced*
*80g mixed baby salad leaves or rocket*
*chips, to serve, optional*

1 Cut each chicken breast fillet in half through the centre to form two thinner fillets. Combine the flours together on one plate and combine the breadcrumbs and parmesan on another. Lightly beat the eggs in a shallow dish. Dip the chicken, one piece at a time, into the flour. Coat in the egg, allowing excess to drain off, then coat both sides with parmesan breadcrumbs, using your fingertips to press the crumbs on.

2 Place onto a tray or plate in a single layer. (Stacking fillets compacts the breadcrumbs, making them moist and unable to crisp up as well when frying.) Cover and refrigerate for 30 minutes if time permits as this helps hold breadcrumbs in place when cooking.

3 Preheat the oven to 150°C fan-forced/170°C no fan. Cover the base of a large non-stick frying pan with oil and heat over medium heat. Cook the chicken in batches for 3 minutes each side or until golden and cooked through. Place on a wire rack over a baking tray and keep warm in the oven.

4 Remove most of the soft white bread from the base and top of each roll. ♥ Spoon the avocado into the base of each roll. Whisk the extra-virgin olive oil and vinegar together in a bowl. Add the tomato and salad leaves and toss gently to coat. Thickly slice the chicken and pile on top of the avocado base. Top with tomato mixture, sandwich together with bread roll top and serve with chips if desired.

♥ Freeze this excess bread and use for soft crumbs in other recipes.

# GOURMET SHEPHERD'S PIE

*Meatloaf and shepherd's pie were two of my dad's favourite meals when I was a child – and they still are. This is for all the dads out there who love the classics.*

SERVES 6

*1kg diced lamb (such as leg or shoulder), trimmed*
*1 tablespoon smoked paprika*
*3 tablespoons olive oil*
*1 brown onion, finely chopped*
*1 tablespoon tomato paste*
*2 cups chicken stock*
*400g can diced tomatoes*
*3 sprigs rosemary, leaves removed*
*1 lemon, quartered*
*1 cup chopped roasted capsicum*
*½ cup black olives, pitted, roughly chopped*
*¼ cup flat leaf parsley, chopped*
*30g tasty cheese, finely grated*

POTATO MASH

*750g desiree or Sebago potatoes, peeled, chopped*
*75g butter, chopped*
*⅓ cup milk*
*⅓ cup thickened cream*

1 Combine the lamb and paprika in a large snap lock bag and shake until well coated. Preheat the oven to 130°C fan-forced./130°C no fan

2 Heat a large stovetop, ovenproof casserole dish over high heat until very hot. Add one tablespoon of the oil, then quickly add half the lamb. Cook for 2–3 minutes, stirring until sealed all over, remove to a plate and repeat with oil and remaining lamb, adding any paprika left in bag.

3 Reduce heat to medium, add the remaining oil and onion and cook, stirring often, for 3 minutes until soft. Add tomato paste and cook for 30 seconds. Stir in the stock, tomatoes and rosemary leaves, then add the lamb and any juices, bringing to a simmer. Poke in the lemon. Cover tightly with a lid or two layers of foil and cook for 3–4 hours or until lamb is tender. ✿

4 For the potato mash, bring potatoes to the boil in a saucepan of salted water over high heat, then boil for 10 minutes or until tender. Drain well, then return the potatoes to the warm saucepan. Shake the saucepan over low heat for 1 minute or until the potatoes look dry. Remove from heat. Roughly mash potatoes with a potato masher. Add butter and mash until well combined. Warm the milk and cream together for 1½ minutes on High/100% in the microwave, then add to the potatoes, beating with a wooden spoon until smooth. Season with salt and pepper.

5 Increase the oven to 200°C fan-forced/220°C no fan. Remove the lemon quarters from the lamb and stir in the capsicum, olives and parsley.

6 Divide the lamb mixture among six 1-cup capacity ovenproof cups or bowls. Top with mashed potato, scatter over the cheese. Place onto a tray and bake 15–20 minutes or until the top is light golden and the lamb piping hot.

✿ You can make the pies to this stage 1–2 days ahead. Keep in an airtight container in the fridge.

# LEMON CAPER FISH WITH FENNEL SALAD

*I have converted many family and friends into fennel fans by serving up this recipe. I think the combination of very finely shaved fennel, the sweetness of raisins and apple and creamy yoghurt is irresistible. Try it – I know you too will be converted.*

SERVES 4

*4 x 150g pieces kingfish fillets or snapper, skin on*
*1 tablespoon extra-virgin olive oil*
*60g butter, chopped*
*1 tablespoon baby capers, rinsed, roughly chopped*
*3 teaspoons seeded mustard*
*1 medium lemon, juiced*
*2 tablespoons chopped chives*

FENNEL SALAD

*1 medium fennel bulb, trimmed, halved lengthways*
*2 Pink Lady apples*
*4 green onions, thinly sliced*
*¼ cup pumpkin seeds, toasted*
*¼ cup muscatels or raisins*
*1 cup mint leaves, roughly chopped*
*¼ cup Greek-style yoghurt*

1 For the fennel salad, thinly slice the fennel and apple (a mandolin is the best way to do this) and place into a bowl. Add the green onions, pumpkin seeds, muscatels and mint. Toss gently to combine. Add the yoghurt, season with salt and pepper and toss to coat.

2 Preheat a medium non-stick frying pan on medium-high heat. Rub both sides of fish fillets with oil and season with salt and pepper. Cook two pieces of fish at a time for 3–4 minutes each side or until just cooked through. Transfer to a plate and cover with foil to keep warm.

3 Reduce the heat to medium, add the butter to the hot pan and swirl until it starts to foam. Add the capers and seeded mustard and cook, stirring, for 1 minute or until butter starts to turn brown. Remove from the heat, add the lemon juice and chives.

4 Place fish onto serving plates, spoon over the sauce and serve with fennel salad.

# BEEF HOTPOT

*Casseroles and wet dishes need to be exceptional in flavour and melt-in-the-mouth tender to get my tick of approval. This one certainly does, plus it's cheap, easy and very satisfying – the dumplings are a bonus when time permits.*

SERVES 6

*2 tablespoons plain flour*
*3 teaspoons ground cumin*
*3 teaspoons ground coriander*
*1 teaspoon smoked paprika*
*1 teaspoon ground turmeric*
*1kg beef (blade, chuck or gravy beef), trimmed, cubed*
*¼ cup olive oil*
*4 rashers bacon, chopped*
*1 large brown onion, finely chopped*
*2 carrots, peeled, diced*
*2 stalks celery, diced*
*2 fresh (or 1 dried) bay leaves*
*400g can diced tomatoes*
*1½ cups beef stock*
*½ cup fresh or frozen peas*

POTATO DUMPLINGS

*350g Desiree or Red Rascal potatoes*
*50g butter, chopped*
*⅔ cup milk*
*1¼ cups self-raising flour, sifted*
*1¼ cups grated tasty cheese*
*¼ cup flat-leaf parsley, chopped*

✿ A casserole dish that can be used on the stovetop and in the oven is a great investment. It's worth saving for a quality brand as it will last a lifetime. If you don't have one, cook steps 1–3 in a frying pan on the stove then transfer to an ovenproof casserole dish.

1 Preheat the oven to 130°C fan-forced/130°C no fan. Combine the flour, cumin, coriander, paprika, turmeric and salt and pepper in a large snap lock bag. Add the beef and shake the bag to coat the beef.

2 Heat an 8–10 cup capacity ovenproof, stovetop casserole dish ✿ on the stovetop over medium-high heat until hot. Add 1 tablespoon of the oil and half the beef and cook, stirring occasionally, for 5 minutes until browned all over. Transfer the beef to a bowl. Repeat with oil and remaining beef, adding any left-over flour and spice mixture.

3 Reduce the heat to medium-low, add the remaining oil and bacon to the hot pan and cook, stirring, for 3 minutes until the bacon starts to colour. Add the onion, carrots, celery and bay leaves and cook a further 5 minutes until the onion is soft. Add the tomatoes and stock, return the beef and any juices in the bowl, then bring to a gentle simmer. Press a piece of baking paper right down onto the surface of the beef – this helps keep it submerged – and cover the dish tightly with a lid or foil. Place into the oven and cook for 3½ hours until tender.

4 With 30 minutes to go, prepare the potato dumplings. Peel and cut the potatoes into large pieces. Place into a shallow microwave-safe dish. Cover with damp paper towel and microwave for 6–7 minutes on High/100% until tender. Drain and transfer the potato to a large mixing bowl. Add the butter and use a potato masher to roughly mash. Add the milk and stir with a wooden spoon until smooth. Add the flour, cheese and parsley and stir until well combined. Season well with salt and pepper.

5 Remove the hotpot from the oven. Increase the oven temperature to 200°C fan-forced/220°C no fan. Remove the lid, discard the baking paper and bay leaves and stir the peas into the hotpot. Divide the dumpling mixture into 12 portions and roll into balls. Drop the dumplings evenly over the hotpot. Bake, uncovered, for 25–30 minutes or until the dumplings are golden and cooked through. Serve.

# MEATLOAF ROLLS WITH BRAISED CABBAGE

*When I close my eyes and think back to when my nan used to make braised cabbage, I remember the terrible smell. That will not happen here – it's sweet, succulent and cooked in minutes. If you can't convince your family, then the meatloaf rolls are awesome served with creamy mash (see recipe page 152).*

SERVES 4

*100g sliced spicy Hungarian salami, chopped*
*4 green onions, chopped*
*½ cup flat-leaf parsley*
*450g pork mince*
*450g chicken mince*
*1 tablespoon Dijon mustard*
*1 cup soft white breadcrumbs*
*1 egg, lightly beaten*
*12 thin slices prosciutto*
*olive oil, for cooking*
*½ bunch thyme*

BRAISED CABBAGE

*1 tablespoon olive oil*
*1 red onion, halved, thinly sliced*
*½ (about 1kg) savoy cabbage, shredded*
*2 tablespoons apple cider vinegar*
*1 cup non-alcoholic sparkling apple cider*
*¼ cup walnuts, toasted, chopped*
*2 tablespoons chopped flat-leaf parsley*

1 Combine the salami, green onions and parsley in a food processor. Process until finely chopped. Add the pork and chicken mince and process until really well combined, almost pasty. Transfer to a large bowl. Add the mustard, breadcrumbs and egg, season with salt and pepper and mix well, using clean hands.

2 Divide the mixture into six portions (about 200g each). Shape each into a 3cm-thick, 12cm-long log. Roll each log tightly in plastic wrap, twisting the ends securely as this will help shape the log. Refrigerate for 1 hour or overnight if time permits.

3 Preheat the oven to 200°C fan-forced/210°C no fan. Remove the meatloaf rolls from the plastic wrap. Wrap two slices of prosciutto around each log, overlapping slightly.

4 Heat a large non-stick frying pan over medium-high heat. Add a little oil and three meatloaf rolls. Cook, turning often, for 3 minutes or until light golden all over. Remove to a tray and repeat with remaining meatloaf rolls. Scatter the thyme over the rolls, then place into the oven. Roast for 15–20 minutes or until cooked through. (The juices should run clear when a skewer is inserted into the centre.)

5 For the braised cabbage, heat the oil in a large, deep frying pan over medium heat. Add onion and cook, stirring, for 5 minutes or until soft. Add the cabbage, vinegar and sparkling apple cider. Cook, uncovered, for 5–10 minutes or until the liquid has evaporated and cabbage is soft. Stir in the walnuts and parsley. Season with salt and pepper. Thickly slice meatloaves if you like and serve warm with cabbage.

# HONEY-MUSTARD BEEF WITH CRISPY POTATO SKINS

*By now you may have realised I love potatoes, especially when served golden, crisp and tender. Choosing the right variety of potato is vital to the dish, which is why I always try to give you a few options for shopping.*

SERVES 4

*6 (160g each) Desiree or Red Rascal potatoes, unpeeled*
*2 tablespoons cornflour or rice flour*
*3 teaspoons Portuguese spice blend*
*vegetable or peanut oil, for deep-frying*
*steamed green beans, to serve*

HONEY-MUSTARD BEEF

*2 tablespoons Dijon mustard*
*1 tablespoon honey*
*1½ tablespoons olive oil*
*2 garlic cloves, crushed*
*1 lemon, rind finely grated, juiced*
*600g rump steak, cut into bite-sized pieces*

1 Preheat the oven to 180°C fan-forced/200°C no fan. Pierce the potatoes all over with a fork and place them directly onto the oven rack, baking for 40 minutes or until just tender when tested with a skewer. Remove the potatoes from the oven and set aside for 15 minutes or until cool enough to handle.

2 Cut the potatoes into quarters lengthways then into thick wedges. Use a teaspoon to remove the potato flesh, leaving half a centimetre of flesh still on the skin. Combine the cornflour and spice blend in a large snap lock bag and shake to combine.

3 Half fill a saucepan or wok with oil and heat over medium-high heat. Add the potato skins to the flour mixture in batches and toss to coat. Deep-fry the potato skins in batches for 2–3 minutes or until golden and crisp. Remove to a wire rack over a tray and keep warm in the oven.

4 For the honey-mustard beef, combine the mustard, honey, oil, garlic, lemon rind and ¼ cup lemon juice in a jug. Whisk until well combined. Pour into a large ceramic dish. Add the beef and stir to coat. Cover and refrigerate 15 minutes if time permits but no longer than 30 minutes.

5 Thread beef onto four skewers. Preheat a barbecue plate on medium-high heat. Barbecue the beef for 6 minutes for medium, turning often, or until cooked to your liking. Serve with crispy potato skins and steamed green beans.

# TRAY-BAKED SAUSAGE WITH CHEESY SCROLLS

SERVES 4

*3 tablespoons olive oil*
*16 chipolata sausages*
*1 leek, halved, washed, thinly sliced*
*3 rashers bacon, rind removed, finely chopped*
*1 carrot, peeled, diced*
*2 sticks celery, diced*
*1 small sweet potato, peeled, chopped*
*400g can lentils or chickpeas, drained, rinsed*
*400g can diced tomatoes*
*1 cup chicken stock*
*¼ cup flat-leaf parsley, chopped*
*½ bunch English spinach* ✿

CHEESY SCROLLS

*1 cup self-raising flour*
*1 cup finely grated tasty cheese*
*40g butter, chilled, chopped*
*100ml milk*

1 Preheat the oven to 200°C fan-forced/210°C no fan. Heat 1 tablespoon of the oil in a large frying pan over medium-high heat. Add half the sausages and cook, turning occasionally, for 3 minutes or until brown all over. Remove to a plate. Repeat with remaining sausages.

2 Reduce heat to medium. Add the remaining oil if needed, then the leek and cook for 4 minutes or until soft. Add the bacon, carrot, celery and sweet potato and cook, stirring often, a further 5 minutes or until vegetables start to soften. Add the lentils, tomatoes and stock, bring to a simmer, then season with salt and pepper. Spoon the mixture into a roasting pan and add the sausages, pressing them into the sauce. Transfer to the oven and cook, uncovered, for 20–30 minutes or until the sweet potato is tender and sausages are cooked through.

3 Meanwhile, for the cheesy scrolls, line a large baking tray with baking paper. Combine the flour, ¼ cup of the cheese and the butter in a food processor. Pulse until combined. Pour in the milk and process to a soft dough. Turn onto a lightly floured surface and knead gently until almost smooth.

4 Roll the dough out to an 18cm x 30cm rectangle. Scatter over the remaining cheese. Roll the dough up firmly like a Swiss roll, starting from one long edge. Cut into 2cm-thick slices and place on a large tray lined with baking paper. Flatten scrolls slightly, then bake on the oven shelf above the sausages for 15–18 minutes or until light golden and cooked through.

5 Stir the parsley and spinach though the sausage bake, top with cheesy scrolls and serve.

✿ *The spinach provides additional vegetables we all need in our daily diet, but if your kids won't eat it, it's fine to leave out.*

# CHORIZO, GOATS' CHEESE & PINE NUT PASTA

*Sometimes in winter you crave creamy, delicious, warming food – this dish will hit the spot. If you're watching the kilojoule count, which most of the time we are, you can replace the cream with stock, and goats' cheese with fresh ricotta. Either way, it's a recipe that I know you will tag as a favourite.*

SERVES 4

*375g fresh lasagna sheets*
*2 tablespoons olive oil*
*500g chorizo sausage, chopped* ✿
*1 red onion, halved, thinly sliced*
*3 free-range eggs*
*150ml thickened cream*
*100g goats' cheese or marinated feta, crumbled*
*¼ cup pine nuts, toasted*
*2 tablespoons flat-leaf parsley, chopped*
*80g baby rocket leaves*
*extra-virgin olive oil, to serve*

1 Tear the pasta sheets into long, irregularly shaped pieces and set aside.

2 Heat the oil in a frying pan over medium-high heat. Add the chorizo and cook, tossing often, for 5 minutes or until it starts to colour. Reduce the heat to medium, add the onion and cook, stirring often, for 4 minutes or until soft. Remove from the heat.

3 Whisk the eggs and cream in a bowl until well combined. Season with salt and freshly ground black pepper.

4 Cook the pasta in a large saucepan of boiling salted water for about 5 minutes or until al dente. Drain the pasta, reserving ⅓ cup of the pasta water. ♥ Return the pasta and 2 tablespoons of the reserved pasta water to the hot saucepan. Quickly add egg mixture and toss over low heat for 1 minute to combine.

5 Remove from the heat, add chorizo mixture, goats' cheese, pine nuts and parsley. Season with plenty of freshly ground black pepper, check the consistency of the sauce, and add more pasta water if required. Pile into warm serving bowls, top with rocket, drizzle with a little oil and serve.

✿ You can buy chorizo raw or cured (already 'cooked'). Both are suitable for this recipe; obviously, the raw will just take a little longer to cook.

♥ The pasta water helps to adjust the consistency of the sauce once the pasta and sauce are combined.

# CRISPY PORK BELLY WITH FIG CHUTNEY

*Though I could eat this more often, it's one of those meats that should be enjoyed 2 to 3 times over winter, and a few more times throughout the year. Don't feel guilty, just enjoy great food!*

SERVES 4-6

*2–2.5kg piece boneless pork belly*
*1 tablespoon fennel seeds*
*4 large garlic cloves*
*2 tablespoons thyme leaves*
*3 tablespoons fine table salt*
*1 lemon, juiced*

FIG CHUTNEY

*250g dried figs, split in half* ✿
*1 cup boiling water*
*400g can apple, chopped*
*¾ cup brown sugar*
*2 tablespoons golden syrup*
*100ml apple cider vinegar*
*¼ teaspoon sea salt flakes, crushed*
*½ teaspoon dried chilli flakes*

✿ The soft, moist, dried figs are best for this recipe.

♥ You can ask your butcher to score the rind.

1 For the fig chutney, roughly chop the figs and place in a heat-proof, microwave-safe bowl, then pour over the boiling water. Microwave, uncovered, for 5 minutes on High/100% or until the figs are soft. (There should still be a little water left in the bowl.) Add the apples, brown sugar, golden syrup, vinegar, salt and chilli. Microwave, uncovered, for 15–20 minutes on High/100%, stirring every 5 minutes, or until chutney has thickened. Spoon the hot chutney into hot sterilised jars and seal. Turn upside down and stand 2 minutes, then turn right side up and allow to cool. Store in the fridge for up to 6 months.

2 Wipe over the pork rind with plenty of paper towel so it's nice and dry. Run an unused razor over the rind to remove any fine hairs. Using a sharp Stanley knife, score the pork rind at about 1cm intervals – this helps crisp the rind but also makes it easy to cut through. ♥

3 Place fennel seeds, garlic, thyme and 2 teaspoons of the salt in a mortar and pound with the pestle until almost smooth. Add 1 tablespoon lemon juice and mix well. Turn the pork belly rind side down. Score the pork almost down to the rind, then rub the garlic mixture over the meat only, avoiding the rind. Turn rind side up and sprinkle with 1 tablespoon of remaining salt. Refrigerate, uncovered, 1 hour or overnight if time permits.

4 Preheat the oven to 230°C fan-forced/240°C no fan. Place the pork, rind side up, on a rack inside a roasting pan. Cover the base of the pan with water. Rub the rind with a little oil and sprinkle generously with remaining salt. Roast for 30 minutes or until the rind is crisp and crackled.

5 Reduce the oven temperature to 140°C fan-forced/150°C no fan and continue cooking for 2 hours or until cooked through. The juices should run clear when a skewer is inserted. Cover loosely with foil and set aside to rest for 20 minutes before slicing and serving with fig chutney and roast beetroot salad (see recipe page 142).

# ROASTED GARLIC & PARMESAN BREAD

*I am no food snob, promise! But I am always disappointed when I see purchased garlic bread on a table – it's not only expensive but it tastes ordinary. It takes no time and requires no skill to make.*

SERVES 6-8

*1 head garlic*
*⅓ cup olive oil*
*1 loaf crusty bread*
*125g butter, softened*
*40g parmesan, finely grated*
*¼ cup flat-leaf parsley, chopped*
*1 lemon, rind finely grated*

1 Preheat the oven to 200°C fan-forced/210°C no fan. Cut the head of garlic in half horizontally to expose the individual cloves. Place cut side up on a sheet of baking paper. Drizzle with 1 tablespoon of the olive oil. Tie the paper up, secure with string. Place into a dish and roast for 15–20 minutes until the garlic is soft. Set aside for 5 minutes to cool, then gently squeeze the garlic flesh onto a board. Use a fork to mash the garlic until smooth. ✿

2 Cut the bread into 2.5cm-thick slices without cutting all the way through. Combine the butter, remaining ¼ cup oil, roasted garlic, parmesan, parsley and lemon rind in a bowl. Season with salt and pepper and mix well.

3 Spread the butter mixture over both sides of each slice of bread. Wrap the loaf in foil, making sure it's secure, folding the foil edges up. ♥ Place onto a tray and bake for 18–20 minutes or until bread is hot. Serve.

The bread can be prepared and frozen before it's baked. When baking from frozen, reduce oven temperature to 180°C fan-forced. It will take about 30 minutes.

✿ If you are stretched for time, ignore this step and replace with 3 cloves crushed garlic – it will still be fabulous!

♥ Folding the foil edges up prevents the butter mixture from running out as it melts and spilling into the oven.

# WINTER SWEET

# APPLE, RHUBARB & CHERRY CRUMBLE

*Sometimes it's the simple things that offer the greatest satisfaction, like a great crumble for dessert. After testing many combinations, this was the hands-down winner!*

SERVES 6

*1 bunch rhubarb, leaves discarded, ends trimmed*
*2 tablespoons white sugar*
*4 Golden Delicious apples, peeled, roughly chopped*
*300g frozen pitted cherries ♥ (Creative Gourmet brand)*
*¾ cup self-raising flour*
*¼ cup plain flour*
*¾ cup brown sugar*
*150g butter, softened*
*¾ cup rolled oats*
*icing sugar, to serve*
*vanilla ice-cream or custard, to serve*

1 Preheat the oven to 180°C fan-forced/200°C no fan. Lightly grease a 6-cup capacity ovenproof dish or six 1-cup capacity ovenproof ramekins.

2 Wash the rhubarb and cut into 3cm pieces. Place onto a shallow, microwave-safe plate, sprinkle over the white sugar and turn to coat all the rhubarb pieces. Cover and microwave for 2–3 minutes on High/100% or until warm. (It should still be firm and hold its shape.) Transfer to a large mixing bowl. Scatter the apple over a large microwave-safe plate, cover and microwave for 3 minutes on High/100% or until warm, then add to the rhubarb. Add the frozen cherries and toss gently to combine all the fruit.

3 Combine the flours, brown sugar and butter in a food processor. Process until the mixture starts to come together. Transfer to a bowl, add the oats and use your fingers to bring the crumble together in coarse chunks.

4 Place the fruit in the greased dish, or divide among the ramekins so they are two-thirds full. Top with the crumble. Place onto a baking tray and bake for 20 minutes or until the topping is crisp and golden. Dust with icing sugar and serve warm with ice-cream or custard.

♥ If you can't find frozen cherries, drain a can of cherries and freeze on a tray for 2 hours.

# PROCESSOR ORANGE CAKE

*This is the easiest, most delicious, moist orange cake ever! Possibly one of my best creations, my family says.*

SERVES 8

*2 (about 220g each) navel oranges, washed ✿*
*185g butter, softened*
*1½ cups caster sugar*
*1 teaspoon vanilla extract*
*3 eggs*
*2¼ cups self-raising flour*

DRIZZLY ORANGE ICING

*½ cup white sugar*
*1 orange, juiced*

1 Preheat the oven to 160°C fan-forced/170°C no fan. Lightly grease a 22cm (base) round springform pan, then line the base with baking paper.

2 Cut the oranges in quarters and discard any seeds. Place the orange quarters, peel and all, into the processor and pulse until roughly chopped. Add the butter, caster sugar and vanilla, pulse until combined – don't worry if the mixture looks curdled. Add the eggs, pulse to combine, then add the flour and pulse until all the flour is distributed. ♥

3 Spoon the mixture into the cake pan and smooth the surface. Bake for 55–60 minutes or until a skewer inserted into the centre comes out clean. Stand in the cake pan for 10 minutes before removing the side and turning onto a wire rack. Turn upright.

4 For the drizzly orange icing, working quickly, combine the white sugar and ¼ cup orange juice in a bowl, then quickly spoon over the warm cake. Set aside to crystallise and cool, though it is also delicious warm.

✿ Navel oranges are perfect for this recipe as they have minimal pith and usually no seeds. The weight is important to the recipe's success and, as they vary considerably throughout the year, be sure you use oranges of similar weight above, even if you need to trim them.

♥ Don't over-process at this stage – just use small bursts of the motor until you no longer see any flour.

# GROWN-UP BROWNIE TRIFLE

*Well-known for my brownies, I have been asked many times via my website for new ways to serve them. After a recent trip to Hawaii with my best friends, this brownie/peanut butter combination was created. Decadent, delicious and naughty.*

MAKES 8

*2 tablespoons Baileys Irish Cream liqueur*
*250g mascarpone*
*1 quantity warm liqueur fudge sauce (see recipe page 112)*
*berries, to serve*

PEANUT BUTTER BROWNIES

*200g butter, chopped*
*200g quality dark chocolate, chopped*
*¼ cup cocoa powder*
*1 cup brown sugar*
*3 eggs, lightly beaten*
*½ cup plain flour*
*¼ cup self-raising flour*
*1 cup roasted macadamia nuts, roughly chopped*
*150g Reece's Peanut Butter Cups, ✿ roughly chopped*

✿ Reece's Peanut Butter Cups are available from most 7-Eleven stores around the country. Alternatively, you can buy them online at www.usafoods.com.au. You can also replace the peanut butter cups with other chocolate bars, like Snickers.

1 Preheat the oven to 180°C no fan. ♥ Grease and line a 3cm-deep, 16.5cm x 26cm (base) slab pan, allowing a 2cm overhang at both long ends so you can then lift the brownie out of the pan when it's cooled.

2 For the peanut butter brownies, combine butter and chocolate in a heat-proof, microwave-safe bowl. Microwave, uncovered, for 2 minutes on High/100%, stirring every minute with a metal spoon until smooth. Stir the cocoa powder into the warm chocolate mixture until the cocoa dissolves. Stir in the sugar and eggs. Sift the flours together over the chocolate mixture and stir to combine. Fold in the macadamia nuts and peanut butter cups.

3 Spread into the prepared pan and bake for 35–40 minutes or until a skewer inserted comes out with moist crumbs sticking to it. Cool completely in the pan.

4 Swirl the Baileys through the mascarpone, then refrigerate until ready to assemble.

5 To assemble, break or chop the brownie into chunks. Arrange some brownie over the base of serving glasses. Top with a dollop of mascarpone, then drizzle with warm fudge sauce. Repeat the layers and serve immediately with berries if desired.

♥ Brownies are not very successful with the oven fan on, because the fan sets the top, forming a crust that prevents the heat from penetrating the centre and baking it through.

# CUSTARD DOUGHNUTS

*Doughnuts are not for every day but, on a cold winter's day, making these with family or friends warms the heart and soul.*

MAKES 40

*½ cup milk*
*4 teaspoons (or 2 x 7g sachets) instant dry yeast* ✿
*pinch of crushed sea salt flakes*
*⅓ cup white sugar*
*3 cups plain flour*
*150g butter, chilled, chopped*
*2 eggs, lightly beaten*
*2 vanilla beans, halved lengthways*
*½ cup caster sugar*
*vegetable, canola, sunflower or light olive oil, for deep-frying*

CUSTARD

*4 egg yolks*
*⅔ cup caster sugar*
*1 teaspoon vanilla bean paste*
*1½ tablespoons plain flour*
*2 tablespoons cornflour*
*2 cups milk*

✿ Dried yeast will keep fresher for longer if stored in the fridge or freezer once opened.

♥ It's important to roll the doughnuts in the sugar as soon as they come from the oil so that the vanilla sugar will stick.

1 For the custard, whisk the egg yolks, sugar, vanilla, plain flour and cornflour together until creamy. Add the milk, ¼ cup at a time, whisking constantly until smooth. Transfer the mixture to a saucepan over medium heat. Cook, stirring constantly, for 10–12 minutes or until the custard just comes to the boil. Pour the hot custard into a heat-proof bowl, press a piece of plastic wrap onto the surface and refrigerate until cold.

2 Warm the milk in a microwave-safe bowl for 20 seconds on High/100%. Add the yeast and stir with a fork until dissolved. Stir in salt and 1 teaspoon of the white sugar. Cover and stand for 10 minutes.

3 Process the flour, butter and remaining white sugar until the mixture resembles fine breadcrumbs. Add the yeast mixture and eggs and pulse to form a soft dough. Turn the dough onto a lightly floured bench top and knead for 10 minutes. Transfer the dough to a lightly oiled bowl and cover with plastic wrap and a tea towel, then stand for 30 minutes.

4 Scrape the soft vanilla seeds from the centre of the bean and place into a snap lock bag. Add the caster sugar and rub vanilla and sugar together until combined, then spread onto a piece of baking paper.

5 Turn the soft dough onto the bench and knead for 1 minute. Roll tablespoons of mixture into balls and place onto a tea towel.

6 Pour oil into a saucepan or wok until one-third full. Heat over medium heat until the oil is hot (about 160C, if you have a thermometer). Cook 6–8 doughnuts at a time for 4–5 minutes, turning or stirring the doughnuts occasionally until a deep golden. Remove the doughnuts from the oil and roll in the vanilla sugar immediately. ♥ Repeat until all the doughnuts are cooked, reheating the oil between batches if necessary.

7 Cut the doughnuts in half with a serrated knife (they tend to split, so this is the best place to cut them) and fill with custard. Serve.

# WHITE CHOCOLATE AND LEMON CURD CHEESECAKE PIE

*To those of you who have my other books, I hope you have made and used the lemon curd many times. Here is another use for this dreamy spread.*

SERVES 6

*200g plain chocolate biscuits (like chocolate ripple)*
*100g butter, melted*
*100g quality white chocolate, chopped*
*375g cream cheese, softened*
*½ cup caster sugar*
*1 egg*
*1 egg yolk*
*150ml sour cream*
*1 cup microwave lemon curd (see recipe page 236)*
*double cream, to serve*

✿ The secret to making cheesecake is not to over-beat – you don't want to introduce air in the mixture.

1 Preheat the oven to 150°C fan-forced/160°C no fan. Lightly grease a 4cm deep, 20cm (base), 25cm (top) pie plate or dish. ♥

2 Process the biscuits to fine crumbs. Add the butter and process until well combined. Press the crumb mixture evenly over the side and base of the pie plate. Refrigerate until ready to fill.

3 Melt the white chocolate in a small heat-proof, microwave-safe bowl, uncovered, in 1-minute bursts on Medium/50%, stirring every minute with a metal spoon until smooth.

4 Use an electric mixer to beat cream cheese and sugar on low speed until smooth and creamy. ✿ Add the melted white chocolate and beat to incorporate. Add the egg then the yolk. Gently fold in the sour cream.

5 Pour the cheesecake mixture over the chilled base and smooth the surface with a spatula. Place on a tray and bake for 40 minutes. (The centre should still wobble.) Turn the oven off, open the oven door slightly and allow the cheesecake to cool completely. Once cooled, refrigerate overnight.

6 Spread the lemon curd over the top of pie. Cut into wedges with a warm knife and serve with cream if desired.

♥ You can double the recipe and bake in a 23cm (base) springform pan for 1 hour. This quantity will feed 10–12.

# MACADAMIA & CHUNKY WHITE CHOCOLATE COOKIES WITH COKE SPIDER

*When the Cookie Man shop first opened in our local shopping centre, they could not keep up with the demand for this variety. I spent many weekends trying to re-create their recipe. Mine have a little more chocolate but, if you know me, you'll have come to expect that!*

MAKES ABOUT 16

*150g butter, softened*
*1 cup brown sugar*
*1 teaspoon vanilla extract*
*½ cup self-raising flour*
*1 cup plain flour*
*½ cup shredded coconut*
*200g quality white chocolate, roughly chopped*
*1/2 cup salted, roasted macadamia nuts, roughly chopped*

COKE SPIDER

*1 can chilled Coke*
*1 scoop vanilla ice-cream*

1 Preheat oven to 170°C fan-forced/180°C no fan. Line two baking trays with baking paper.

2 Using an electric mixer, beat the butter, brown sugar and vanilla until just combined. Sift the flours together over the butter mixture and stir until well combined. Stir in the coconut, white chocolate and macadamia nuts.

3 Squash a heaped spoonful of the cookie dough together in your hand until it comes together, ♥ place onto the prepared trays and flatten a little with your fingertips, allowing room for spreading. Bake for 15–20 minutes or until light golden. When they come out of the oven, use a large flat spatula to carefully press the top of each cookie down a little. ✿ Allow to cool completely on the trays before serving (if you can resist, as they are sensational warm).

4 For the spider, pour the Coke into a chilled glass to no more than two-thirds full, add the ice-cream and stir gently until the spider begins to froth. Serve immediately with cookies.

✿ You don't have to flatten the top here if you don't want to – I find this produces a slightly fudgier cookie in the centre.

♥ The dough may seem a little dry, but as you squash it the warmth of your hand will make it come together and bake to perfection.

# PEAR & GINGER SYRUP DUMPLINGS

*When I made these last year on* Ready Steady Cook, *everyone went nuts and I ended up making more for our crew out the back during our break. It was one of the most-requested recipes of the season.*

SERVES 6

*40g butter*
*2½ tablespoons golden syrup*
*50ml thickened cream*
*1 tablespoon grated fresh ginger* ♥
*1 cup self-raising flour*
*2 firm Beurre Bosc pears, peeled, grated, excess juice squeezed out*
*thickened cream, to serve*
*60g glacé ginger, finely chopped, optional*
*honey-roasted pears, to serve (see recipe page 124)*

SYRUP

*2 cups warm water*
*⅔ cup golden syrup*
*1 cup brown sugar*
*60g butter, chopped*

1 Combine all the syrup ingredients in a heat-proof, microwave-safe jug and microwave, uncovered, on High/100% for 2–3 minutes until the butter has melted and the syrup is warm. Pour the syrup evenly between two medium (about 22–23cm base) shallow frying pans ✿ and bring the syrup to a gentle simmer over medium heat.

2 Meanwhile, melt the butter and golden syrup together, then pour into a bowl. Stir in the cream and fresh ginger. Sift the flour over the ginger mixture and stir to form a thick batter, then fold in the pear.

3 Drop three large spoonfuls of batter into each pan of simmering syrup, allowing room for spreading. Cover and cook for 3 minutes, then carefully turn the dumplings over and cook for a further 2–3 minutes until cooked through. Drizzle over cream, scatter over the crystallised ginger ♥ and serve with honey-roasted pears if desired.

✿ I divide the syrup into two pans because when you drop the raw dumplings into the simmering syrup, it's the flour in the dumplings that thicken the syrup and transforms it into a sauce. I find if you cook the two batches of dumplings in one pan, the second batch is tough and heavy because the syrup has thickened from cooking the first batch.

♥ You can omit the ginger if you don't like it – the dumplings are still delicious.

# CHOCOLATE FRENCH BRIOCHE TOAST

*To say I grew up on chocolate and brioche for weekend breakfast would highlight just how spoilt I was. My nan would always create wonderful delights, and those are treasured memories that will live with me forever.*

MAKES 6

*6 x 1.5cm-thick slices brioche bread ♥*
*1 cup chocolate hazelnut spread (see recipe page 247)*
*3 eggs*
*150ml milk*
*1 teaspoon vanilla bean paste*
*50g ghee or unsalted butter ✿*
*icing sugar, to serve*

1 Preheat the oven to 180°C fan-forced/200°C no fan. Cut each slice of brioche in half crossways and place on a board. Spread half the slices very thickly with chocolate spread and sandwich together with the other brioche half, pressing down gently to secure.

2 Whisk the eggs, milk and vanilla together with a fork in a wide, shallow bowl.

3 Melt half the ghee or butter in a large non-stick frying pan over medium heat until hot. Dip 2 sandwiches, one at a time, into the egg mixture to coat. Allow the excess to drain, then lower into the hot pan. Cook for 3–4 minutes each side or until golden. Transfer to a wire rack and keep warm in the oven while cooking the remaining sandwiches in the remaining ghee or butter.

4 Dust the hot toast with icing sugar and serve.

✿ I use ghee quite a lot when pan-frying as it doesn't burn as quickly as butter.

♥ Brioche is a sweet, buttery European-style bread available from specialty food shops and bakeries. It's worth tracking it down, but panettone or fruit loaf are great alternatives.

# FIG & WALNUT PASTE WITH OLIVE DAMPER

*I just love the fig and date pastes you can buy and serve on a cheese platter or with some fresh pears for dessert. They're very expensive, so I have finally developed this inexpensive, easy, foolproof recipe.*

SERVES 6

*250g soft dried figs, roughly chopped*
*75g dried apple or pear, roughly chopped*
*1 cup cold tap water*
*2 teaspoons ground cinnamon*
*1 cup white sugar*
*1 cup walnuts, chopped*
*buffalo mozzarella, to serve*

OLIVE DAMPER

*3 cups self-raising flour*
*1 teaspoon sea salt flakes*
*80g butter, chilled, cubed*
*4 sprigs rosemary*
*180g marinated olives, pitted, roughly chopped*
*¾ cup milk*

♥ The fig paste will keep for 3–4 months in the fridge well wrapped in baking paper and stored in an airtight container.

1 Combine the figs, apple or pear and water in a medium saucepan over medium heat. Bring to simmer and cook for 5–7 minutes, stirring occasionally, until the fruit is soft and pulpy and the water has been almost absorbed. Remove from heat, cover and stand for 5 minutes.

2 Stir the cinnamon into the warm fruit. Transfer the mixture to a food processor and process until almost smooth. Scrape the mixture into a large heat-proof, microwave-safe bowl and stir in the white sugar. Microwave, uncovered, for 12 minutes on High/100%, stirring every 3 minutes until the paste is thick. Fold in the walnuts.

3 Spoon the hot fig paste into a log shape on a large sheet of baking paper, rolling up and twisting the ends to form a tight roll. Set aside at room temperature for 1 hour, then refrigerate overnight until firm. ♥

4 For the olive damper, preheat the oven to 200°C fan-forced/220°C no fan. Dust a baking tray with a little extra flour. Combine the flour, salt and butter in a food processor. Process to fine crumbs, then transfer the mixture to a large bowl. Remove leaves from 1 sprig of rosemary and stir into the flour with the olives. Make a well in the centre, add the milk and use a table knife to stir until the dough just comes together, adding a little more milk if necessary. Use your hands to bring the dough together.

5 Turn the dough onto a lightly floured surface and divide the mixture into 6 portions (each about 150g). Knead gently until the base is smooth, then shape each into a 7cm round. Place onto the tray, allowing room for spreading. Use a sharp knife to mark a cross on top of each. Cut the remaining rosemary sprigs into 7cm lengths and insert one sprig into the centre of each damper. Bake for 25–30 minutes or until the damper is cooked through. (It should sound hollow when tapped on the base.) Serve warm with fig paste and buffalo mozzarella.

# SPRING

*Tulips in full bloom, farmers' markets coming alive, fresh berries in abundance, planting fresh herbs, picnics, barbecues and beach parties every weekend remind me spring has sprung.*

# BEST BUYS

## FRUIT

### SEPTEMBER

*apples:*
  *Lady Williams*
*bananas*
*berries:*
  *strawberries*
*grapefruit:*
  *yellow and ruby red*
*lemons:*
  *Lisbon*
*mandarins:*
  *Ellendale*
*melons:*
  *rockmelon*
*oranges:*
  *navel and blood*
*pineapple*
*rhubarb*

### OCTOBER

*bananas*
*berries:*
  *strawberries*
*grapefruit:*
  *yellow and ruby red*
*lemons:*
  *Lisbon*
*mangoes:*
  *Kensington Pride*
*melons:*
  *rockmelon and watermelon*
*mulberries*
*oranges:*
  *Valencia*
*papaya and papaw*
*pineapple*
*rhubarb*

### NOVEMBER

*bananas*
*berries:*
  *strawberries, boysenberries, blueberries and mulberries*
*coconuts*
*grapefruit:*
  *ruby red*
*mangoes:*
  *Kensington Pride*
*melons:*
  *rockmelon, watermelon and honeydew*
*oranges:*
  *Valencia*
*papaya and papaw*
*passionfruit*
*peaches:*
  *Clingstone Yellow*
*pineapple*
*rhubarb*

# VEGETABLES

## SEPTEMBER

*Asian greens*
*asparagus:*
*green and white*
*avocados:*
*Hass*
*beans:*
*green*
*beetroot*
*cabbage:*
*Chinese*
*cauliflower*
*chillies*
*fennel:*
*baby*
*garlic*
*ginger*
*leeks*
*onions*
*parsnip*
*peas*
*pumpkin:*
*butternut and Queensland blue*
*radishes*
*spinach*
*tomatoes*
*watercress*

## OCTOBER

*Asian greens*
*asparagus:*
*green and white*
*avocados*
*Hass*
*beans:*
*green and broad*
*beetroot*
*cabbage:*
*Chinese*
*capsicum:*
*red, green and yellow*
*cauliflower*
*chillies*
*garlic*
*leeks*
*onions*
*peas*
*pumpkin:*
*butternut*
*radishes*
*spinach*
*tomatoes*
*watercress*

## NOVEMBER

*Asian greens*
*asparagus:*
*green and white*
*avocados:*
*Hass*
*beans:*
*green*
*beetroot*
*cabbage:*
*Chinese*
*capsicum:*
*red, green and yellow*
*celery*
*chillies*
*corn*
*garlic*
*leeks*
*lettuce*
*onions*
*peas*
*radishes*
*rhubarb*
*tomatoes*
*watercress*
*zucchini*

# PRODUCE

## WATERMELON

A wedge of icy-cold watermelon, a glass of watermelon juice or a scoop of watermelon sorbet – all delicious options for this magnificent fruit.

Seedless watermelon is a hybrid variety that contains no black seeds but does have soft, white, edible seeds. Watermelon deteriorates around the seeds first, so the seedless variety has a longer shelf life.

*Storage*: Choose melons that sound hollow when tapped. Store out of direct sunlight for up to two weeks. Once cut, cover and keep in the fridge for up to 3 days.

*Best buddies with*: Prawns, chicken, duck and ham; fresh-ground and glacé ginger; soft white cheese, like ricotta, feta and goats' curd; mint, strawberries, lime and vodka.

## BERRIES

The sight and sweet aroma of fresh berries in the shops gets my mouth salivating and imagination bursting with ideas. The new varieties and varied climate around the country sees berries readily available for longer stretches of time than ever before.

Strawberries: Rated as most people's favourite fruit. Size and colour are not true indicators of flavour – bigger does not always mean better. Try to smell the fruit; an intense fragrance is a good indicator of flavour.

Blueberries: They should have a deep-blue skin colour, covered in a glossy, waxy-white 'bloom'. They are full of antioxidants, so they not only taste great raw and cooked but are rated as a 'super food'.

Raspberries: Sweet and juicy, this heavenly fruit is delicious raw or cooked. Like all berries, they are picked by hand, which is why we pay more per kilo than all other fruit.

Blackberries: Plump and round, the many bead-like segments that make up the fruit are firm and full of juice. They make fabulous pies, tarts and jams.

Boysenberries: A hybrid fruit of blackberries crossed with raspberries and loganberries. Slightly larger, more elongated and redder in colour than the blackberry, they are sweeter and juicier as well.

*Storage*: Berries are highly perishable. Open the punnet and check that there are no soft or damaged berries – discard them as they will encourage the speedy deterioration of the remaining berries. Place unwashed berries (water will speed up deterioration) onto a paper towel-lined plate, cover loosely with paper towel then plastic wrap. Store on the lowest shelf in the fridge and eat within 2 days.

*Best buddies with*: Sugar, honey and maple syrup; cream, sour cream and crème fraîche; vanilla; ricotta and feta; citrus and passionfruit; almonds, chocolate; pastry.

## PINEAPPLE

Often overlooked because it's too fiddly to peel. Don't let this put you off this wonderful, exotic fruit.

Smooth-leaf is the most common variety and available all year round. During the summer months, one-third of the skin should be golden. During the cooler months, try to purchase ones where more than half the skin is golden. This variety has a tough central core that needs to be removed. Extremely juicy, they are well-suited for cooking, juicing and eating fresh.

Roughy or rough-leaf varieties are small fruit with rough, serrated leaves. They are very sweet. The flesh is drier compared to smooth-leaf, which makes them less suitable for juicing but perfect for use in baking and salsas.

Mareeba Gold is a new variety. It's easy to recognise as it comes without the leaf top. Low acid, sweet and juicy with a soft, edible core. Great juiced, used in fruit salads and salsas, and makes great jam and chutney.

*Storage*: Pineapples have a short shelf life; after harvesting they bruise easily. Store in a fruit bowl at room temperature for 1–2 days. Alternatively, place whole fruit in a storage bag, leaving the leaves exposed, for up to 3 days. Peeled and cut fruit will keep in a glass or Pyrex airtight container for up to 1 week.

*Tip*: Pineapples contain a protein-destroying enzyme called bromelin, which prevents gelatine from setting, causes meat to break down and sour cream and yoghurt to weep. When adding pineapple to salads containing dairy, do so just before serving.

*Best buddies with*: Palm sugar, brown sugar and maple syrup; bananas, lychee, lime and mango; cream and butter; nutmeg and vanilla; rum and brandy; white rice; pork and ham; prawns and white fish; pistachio kernels.

## PEAS

As a child, shelling fresh peas with my nan wasn't enough to encourage me to eat them – they were the one vegetable I would leave on my plate. The good news is I love them now and they feature on my table regularly.

Podded green peas, as the name suggests, are the peas inside the pod. To shell, run your thumbnail along the seam of the pod to split it open, remove the peas and discard the pod. Steamed, microwaved or sautéed, they are fabulous in risotto and pasta dishes. About 350g fresh peas in the pod will give you 1 cup shelled peas.

Snow peas are eaten whole. They do, however, require the removal of the strings that run along either side of the pod. Snow pea sizes reflect their age, so the smaller they are the younger and often sweeter they are. They're best stir-fried but don't overlook serving them raw, shredded in salads, wraps and rice paper rolls. The leaves from snow peas are sold as snow pea tendrils. When you see them, buy them and use as you would baby spinach or rocket.

Sugar snap peas, like snow peas, are eaten whole once the string that runs along the flat side of the pod has been removed. They're harvested while the pods are still young and tender, before the peas inside have fully matured. They're best cooked in a stir-fry, steamed or microwaved.

*Best buddies with*: Rice and pasta; butter and olive oil; cream and fresh ricotta; potatoes, onion, leek and garlic; chicken, bacon and ham; mint, sage, parsley and bay leaves; eggs and cream; prawns.

## ASPARAGUS

Spring rain and sunshine is responsible for the bulk of this stunning vegetable.

Green and white asparagus is the same variety. The green colour comes from exposure to sunlight. When the tips are about 20cm above the soil, the spears are cut. A common misconception is that thin spears are younger and more tender. In fact, long, thick, dark-green spears with tightly closed heads are considered by experts as the best quality.

White asparagus has long been considered a scarce delicacy – and commands double the price of green asparagus because the production costs are high. They're harvested while the spear is still below ground.

Purple asparagus has a deep, fruity flavour. With a twenty per cent higher sugar content than green asparagus, purple asparagus has a hint of sweetness and is delicious shredded and served raw in salads.

*Storage*: Wrap bunches in a clean, damp tea towel, then store in a plastic bag in the fridge crisper for up to 4–5 days.

*Best buddies with*: Butter and olive oil; eggs, cream and cheese; – bread; Dijon mustard; parsley, chives, tarragon and thyme; lemon and oranges; soy; ham, bacon and chicken; fresh, smoked.

## CAPSICUM

Colourful, versatile and nutritious, capsicums are highly prized in all cuisines from Indian and Greek to Thai and Hungarian.

Capsicums are usually sold by colour. While the green ones are available all year round, it's spring when the sweet, coloured varities are plentiful and cheaper. All capsicum are green at first. Allowed to ripen, they then turn red, orange, yellow or a purple-black. Red capsicums are the sweetest due to their higher sugar content.

*Storage*: Keep capsicums in a sealed plastic bag in the fridge crisper for up to 1 week.

*Best buddies with*: Shallots, onion, garlic and chilli; olive oil; olives, capers and anchovies; chicken, fish and seafood; tomatoes and eggplant; parsley, basil and rosemary; feta, goats' curd, parmesan and mozzarella.

# SPRING SAVOURY

# SOUFFLÉ OMELETTE WITH WORCESTERSHIRE MUSHROOMS

*This is a great breakfast, lunch or light dinner dish. Mushrooms and Worcestershire sauce are perfect partners.*

SERVES 2

*4 eggs, separated*
*2 tablespoons milk*
*4 green onions, thinly sliced*
*¼ cup flat-leaf parsley, chopped*
*2 tablespoons chopped chives*
*30g butter, chopped*
*60g mozzarella, grated* ✿
*hot buttered toast, to serve*

WORCESTERSHIRE MUSHROOMS

*30g butter, chopped*
*200g button mushrooms, thinly sliced*
*1 tablespoon Worcestershire sauce*

1 For the Worcestershire mushrooms, melt the butter in a large frying pan over medium-high heat until foaming. Add the mushrooms and cook, tossing often, until the mushrooms are light golden and tender. Add the Worcestershire sauce and toss to combine. Keep warm.

2 Meanwhile, preheat grill over medium heat. Using a fork, beat the egg yolks, milk, green onions, parsley, chives and a little freshly ground black pepper in a medium bowl until well combined. In a separate bowl, use an electric hand mixer to beat the egg whites to soft peaks. Fold the egg whites into the herb–egg mixture.

3 Melt the butter in a medium (about 22cm base) oven-proof frying pan over medium heat. Pour in the omelette mixture, reduce heat to low and cook uncovered for 2–3 minutes until golden underneath. Top with half the cheese, then place under the hot grill for 2–3 minutes until cheese is melted. Spoon the mushrooms over half the omelette, top with remaining cheese, then fold the omelette over to cover the mushrooms. Slide onto a plate, cut in half and serve with hot buttered toast.

✿ I prefer to buy a round of mozzarella and grate it myself – pre-grated ones contain all sorts of chemicals I prefer not to consume. To store unused block, wrap it tightly in greaseproof paper then plastic and store in an airtight container.

# PRAWN AVOCADO & ANTIPASTO BAGUETTE

*These are awesome packed for lunch boxes or a picnic or lightly toasted for a light meal on a warm, balmy spring or summer's night. I say this feeds 4 but everyone at the photography shoot convinced me it feeds more.*

SERVES 6–8

*4 x 36cm-long thin baguettes*
*4 tablespoons whole egg mayonnaise*
*1 large firm ripe avocado, mashed*
*800g medium cooked king prawns, peeled, deveined*
*1 cup chopped antipasto (see recipe page 20)*
*50g snow pea tendrils or baby rocket or spinach* ✿

1 Slice the baguettes in half lengthways, leaving them attached along one long edge. Combine the mayonnaise and avocado and spoon evenly between each baguette.

2 Using a small sharp knife split the prawns in half down the centre. Toss the prawns with the antipasto and snow pea tendrils, season with salt and freshly ground black pepper. Divide the mixture between the baguettes and serve.

✿ Snow pea tendrils taste as good as they look. They are a greengrocer line, not a supermarket one (but it won't take long for them to catch on).

# SHREDDED SNOW PEA SALAD WITH CRISPY-SKIN SALMON

*Quick, easy, light and healthy – this recipe ticks all the boxes for a perfect mid-week spring meal.*

SERVES 4

*100g rice vermicelli noodles*
*4 x 125g pieces salmon, skin on*
*olive oil cooking spray*
*1 long green chilli, halved, deseeded*
*1 stick lemongrass, white part roughly chopped*
*2 garlic cloves, roughly chopped*
*1½ tablespoons peanut oil*
*400g snow peas, topped, shredded*
*½ small lemon, juiced*
*1 tablespoon fish sauce*
*2 teaspoons honey*
*½ cup mint leaves, shredded*
*lime wedges, to serve*

1 Place the noodles in a large heat-proof bowl. Cover with plenty of boiling water and set aside for 3–5 minutes or until just tender. Drain well, refresh in cold water, then drain well again and set aside.

2 Heat a barbecue plate or char-grill pan on high. Spray both sides of the salmon with oil and season with salt and pepper. Barbecue skin side down for 3–4 minutes until crisp. Turn and barbecue for 1 minute for medium, or until cooked to your liking. Transfer the salmon to a plate and cover with foil to keep warm. Set aside for 5 minutes to rest.

3 Pound the chilli, lemongrass, garlic and 2 teaspoons of the peanut oil in a mortar with the pestle to a paste, or process in a small food processor.

4 Heat a wok or frying pan over medium heat until hot. Add the remaining oil and lemongrass mixture and stir-fry 1 minute until aromatic. Add the snow peas and cook for 1 minute. Remove from the heat and pour over the combined lemon juice, fish sauce and honey. Toss to coat.

5 Add the warm snow pea mixture and mint to the noodles and toss to combine. Pile onto serving plates and serve with salmon and lime wedges.

# LAMB KEBABS

*I had these amazing kebabs at a cute little mobile trolley just near Eumundi markets on Queensland's Sunshine Coast. The Turkish lady tried to explain how to make them as best she could, and from there I have been experimenting to mirror my experience.*

SERVES 4

*2 brown onions, chopped*
*1 large lemon, juiced*
*2 garlic cloves, crushed*
*2 teaspoons sweet paprika*
*¼ teaspoon chilli powder*
*½ teaspoon ground cumin*
*¼ cup olive oil*
*800g lamb loin backstrap, cut into 4cm chunks*
*1 cup Greek-style yoghurt*
*8 slices Turkish bread, toasted*
*tabouli, to serve*

JALAPEÑO HUMMOS

*400g can chickpeas, rinsed, drained*
*2 tablespoons sliced, pickled jalapeño chillies, drained* ♥
*2 tablespoons tahini*
*1 garlic clove, crushed*
*60ml extra-virgin olive oil*
*1 lemon, juiced*

1 Combine the onion, ¼ cup lemon juice, garlic, paprika, chilli powder, cumin and oil in a food processor or blender. Process or blend until smooth. Strain the marinade into a ceramic dish, discarding the solids. Add the lamb to the marinade and turn to coat. Cover and refrigerate for 2–4 hours if time permits.

2 For the jalapeño hummos, combine all the ingredients in a food processor. Process until smooth, transfer to a bowl, taste and season with salt and pepper.

3 Swirl ⅓ cup jalapeño hummos through the yoghurt. Cover and refrigerate for 2 hours. Press a piece of plastic wrap onto the surface of the remaining hummos and refrigerate for another use.

4 Remove the lamb from the marinade and thread onto four metal skewers.

5 Preheat a barbecue plate or grill on high heat. Add the lamb and cook, turning occasionally, for 6–8 minutes for medium or until cooked to your liking. Transfer to a plate, cover and allow to stand 5 minutes. Serve the kebab with jalapeño hummos yoghurt, toasted Turkish bread and tabouli.

♥ You will find jalapeño chillies in a jar near the olives at your supermarket.

# CHILLI JAM LAMB

*Spring is the perfect time of year to indulge yourself and the family in good Aussie lamb weekly. Since there is more available at this time of year watch for the prices to drop. When they do, try this.*

SERVES 4

*2 tablespoons olive oil*
*1 small brown onion, finely chopped*
*1 garlic clove, crushed*
*100g goats' cheese, crumbled*
*2 tablespoons flat-leaf parsley, chopped*
*8 double lamb cutlets*
*¼ cup chilli jam*
*2 tablespoons rosemary leaves*
*barbecued flatbread, to serve*
*red salad, to serve (see recipe page 32)*

CHILLI JAM ✿

*6 red Birdseye chillies, seeds in, roughly chopped*
*4 large red banana chillies, seeds removed, roughly chopped*
*1 small red onion, peeled, chopped*
*3 large garlic cloves, crushed*
*½ cup cold tap water*
*1 teaspoon sea salt flakes*
*2 cups white sugar*
*½ cup red wine vinegar*
*⅓ cup port or sherry*

1 For the chilli jam, place all the chillies, onion, garlic, water and salt into a food processor. Process until finely chopped. Transfer to a 12-cup capacity, heat-proof, microwave-safe bowl. Stir in the sugar, vinegar and port. Microwave, uncovered, for 3 minutes on High/100%, stirring every minute or until sugar has dissolved. Microwave, uncovered, for a further 20–25 minutes on High/100% or until the jam reaches setting point (see tip on page 67). Spoon hot jam into hot sterilised jars and seal. Turn upside down for 2 minutes. Turn upright and allow to cool .

2 Heat 1 tablespoon of the oil in a small frying pan over medium heat. Add the onion and garlic and cook for 4 minutes or until onion softens. Transfer to a bowl and set aside to cool for 15 minutes. Add the goats' cheese and parsley. Season with freshly ground black pepper.

3 Cut a pocket into each double lamb cutlet. Fill with a spoonful of goats' cheese mixture. Combine the chilli jam, rosemary and remaining oil then brush all over the lamb. Cover and refrigerate 30 minutes if time permits.

4 Preheat a barbecue plate or grill on medium heat. Barbecue the lamb for 8–10 minutes for medium, turning to cook all sides, or until cooked to your liking. Transfer to a tray, cover and set aside to rest for 10 minutes. Serve with barbecued flatbread and red salad.

✿ Once opened, store chilli jam in the fridge for up to 3 months.

# CHICKEN FATTOUCHE SALAD

*Traditionally, this recipe uses flatbread, but it is one of my go-to recipes to use up stale bread, which is why my recipe calls for sourdough.*

SERVES 4

*4 tablespoons olive oil*
*½ lemon, juiced*
*2 chicken breast fillets, trimmed*
*1 teaspoon sumac spice*
*4 thick slices stale sourdough bread*
*2 Lebanese cucumbers, quartered lengthways, deseeded*
*350g fresh peas, shelled* ✿
*4 green onions, thinly sliced*
*4 radishes, scrubbed, thinly sliced*
*250g cherry tomatoes, halved*
*½ cup flat-leaf parsley leaves*
*¼ cup mint leaves*
*80g Greek feta*

DRESSING

*½ lemon, juiced*
*4 tablespoons extra-virgin olive oil*
*½ garlic clove, crushed*
*pinch sumac spice*

1 Preheat oven to 180°C fan-forced/200°C no fan. Combine 2 tablespoons olive oil, lemon juice and salt and pepper in a ceramic dish. Add chicken and turn to coat. Cover and refrigerate for no longer than 15 minutes.

2 Combine the sumac with the remaining oil and brush over both sides of each piece of bread, then tear into chunks. Place onto a tray and bake for 5 minutes or until crisp. Roughly chop the cucumber.

3 Preheat a large non-stick frying pan on medium-high heat. Drain the chicken then add to the hot pan and cook for 4–5 minutes each side or until just cooked through. Remove to a board, cover and allow to stand for 10 minutes. Add the shelled peas to the hot pan and cook, shaking the pan, for 1 minute. Remove from the heat and set aside. Thinly slice the chicken.

4 Combine the crisp bread, cucumber, green onions, radishes, tomatoes, parsley, mint, peas and chicken in a large bowl, tossing gently to combine. Scatter the salad over a platter. Crumble over the feta, then season with lots of freshly ground black pepper.

5 Combine all the dressing ingredients in a screw-top jar and shake well to combine. Pour the dressing over the salad at the table and serve.

✿ 350g fresh peas should give you about 1 cup shelled peas.

# FLAT-ROASTED SPATCHCOCK

*Marinating chicken after it's been cooked is a technique I only recently learned, and it's one I love using. Wait until you taste this – roast chicken will never be boring again.*

SERVES 4

*4 x 500g fresh spatchcock*
*2 tablespoons extra-virgin olive oil*
*½ bunch thyme*
*fig, pear and fennel salad, to serve (see recipe page 108)*

HERB SAUCE

*⅓ cup whole almonds, skin on*
*½ cup walnuts*
*1 small garlic clove*
*½ cup firmly packed flat-leaf parsley*
*½ cup firmly packed basil leaves*
*2 teaspoons caster sugar*
*¼ cup extra-virgin olive oil*
*2 tablespoons apple cider vinegar*

1 Preheat the oven to 200°C fan-forced/220°C no fan. Place spatchcock, breast side down, on board. Cut either side of the backbone. Discard the backbone, ♥ turn bird over and press down on the breast to flatten. Pat dry with paper towel.

2 Rub the olive oil all over the skin side of the spatchcock. Season well with salt and pepper. Place in a single layer in a lightly greased roasting pan. Scatter over the thyme sprigs and roast for 30 minutes or until cooked through.

3 To make the herb sauce, combine almonds, walnuts, garlic, parsley, basil and sugar in a food processor. Process until roughly chopped. With motor running, add oil slowly until all is incorporated. Transfer to a bowl, stir in the vinegar and season with salt and pepper.

4 Spoon the herb sauce over the warm spatchcock and serve with fig, pear and fennel salad.

♥ The backbones make great chicken stock. Keep them in a container in the freezer until you have 12 – they will make 4 cups of stock.

# WARM DUCK SALAD WITH POMEGRANATE DRESSING

*Duck used to be gourmet, but it's easy to find in many supermarkets and greengrocers that carry deli lines. The meat's richness means you don't need as much to feel satisfied.*

SERVES 4

*4 (100g each) boneless duck breast fillets, skin on*
*100g mixed baby salad leaves*
*½ cup mint leaves*
*2 stalks celery, thinly sliced*
*2 oranges, peeled, segmented*
*1 cup bean sprouts, trimmed*
*½ cup roasted peanuts, roughly chopped*
*crusty bread, to serve*

POMEGRANATE DRESSING

*2 tablespoons pomegranate molasses*
*1 tablespoon freshly squeezed orange juice*
*3 tablespoons extra-virgin olive oil*
*1 teaspoon finely grated ginger*

POMEGRANATE MOLASSES ✿

*1 cup pomegranate juice*
*⅓ cup white sugar*
*1 lemon, juiced*

1 To make the pomegranate molasses, combine all the ingredients in a small saucepan over a medium heat. Stir occasionally until the sugar has dissolved. Bring to a gentle boil, then continue to boil for 15–20 minutes until syrup has reduced to ½ cup (it will thicken upon cooling). Pour into a clean jar, allow to cool, then secure a lid and refrigerate.

2 Score the skin of the duck breasts in a diamond pattern, then season well with salt and pepper. Heat a large non-stick frying pan over medium-high heat until hot. Add duck, skin side down, and cook for 5 minutes or until golden. Turn over and cook for 5–6 minutes for medium. Remove the pan from the heat. Cover and allow the duck to rest in the warm pan for 10 minutes.

3 For the pomegranate dressing, combine all the ingredients and salt and pepper in a screw-top jar. Shake well to combine.

4 While the duck is warm, slice and place into a shallow dish, pour over half the dressing and turn to coat both sides of the warm duck.

5 Combine the salad leaves, mint, celery, orange segments and bean sprouts in a large shallow bowl. Top with duck and any juices, drizzle over the remaining dressing, scatter over the peanuts and serve with crusty bread.

✿ Pomegranate molasses is expensive to buy, but quick, easy and inexpensive to make. It will keep indefinitely in a sterilised jar in the fridge.

# VEAL SALTIMBOCCA

*Spring is by far the best time to eat and enjoy veal – and there is no better way than saltimbocca. A little bit of gnocchi on the side to soak up all those delicious pan juices – bellissimo!*

SERVES 4

*375g cherry tomatoes, on the vine*
*olive oil cooking spray*
*4 large uncrumbed veal escalopes, cut in half crossways*
*8 small sage leaves*
*8 slices prosciutto*
*2 tablespoons olive oil*
*40g butter*
*½ cup chicken stock or white wine*
*potato gnocchi, cooked to serve*

1 Preheat the oven to 230°C fan-forced/240°C no fan. Arrange the tomatoes on a baking tray lined with baking paper. Spray lightly with oil and season with salt and freshly ground black pepper. Roast for 5 minutes or until the tomato skins start to split. Remove from the oven and set aside.

2 Place each piece of veal between plastic wrap and pound with a meat mallet until about 5mm thick. Season with salt and pepper. Place a sage leaf in the centre of each piece of veal, then wrap a piece of prosciutto around the veal to hold the sage in place. Secure with a toothpick if necessary.

3 Heat a shallow frying pan over medium-high heat until hot. Add the oil and half the butter and swirl until melted. Cook the veal in batches for 1–2 minutes each side, transfer to a plate and cover to keep warm.

4 Add the stock or wine to the hot pan and bring to a boil, scraping up bits on the bottom of the pan. Reduce the heat to medium and simmer for 3–4 minutes until liquid reduces slightly. Add the remaining butter and shake the pan gently over the heat until the sauce is smooth.

5 Place the veal onto serving plates, spoon over the sauce and serve with tomatoes and gnocchi.

# STEAK WITH BALSAMIC MUSHROOMS

*Okay, it may sound like a weird combination but trust me – sweet, sticky, salty mushrooms are just perfect with pan-seared steak.*

SERVES 4

*¼ cup orange marmalade*
*1 tablespoon balsamic vinegar*
*3 tablespoons olive oil*
*300g button or Swiss brown mushrooms*
*2 (about 300g each) porterhouse steaks* ♥
*dressed leaves, like snow pea tendrils, rocket or spinach and lemon wedges, to serve*

CRISPY BAKED CHIPS

*500g Red Rascal or Pontiac potatoes*
*50g butter, melted*
*sprigs of fresh thyme*

1 For the crispy baked chips, preheat the oven and baking tray to 200°C fan-forced/220°C no fan. Thinly slice the unpeeled potatoes using a mandolin. Place into a bowl of water and stand for 5 minutes. Drain well then pat potatoes dry using plenty of paper towel. Place in bowl, pour over the butter and toss to coat. Lightly grease the hot tray in the oven, then spread potatoes onto the tray no more than three layers deep. Scatter over the thyme and roast for 20–25 minutes until tender and golden.

2 Meanwhile, combine the marmalade, balsamic and 2 tablespoons of the olive oil in a large bowl. Add mushrooms and toss to coat.

3 Heat a large frying pan over medium-high heat until hot. Brush the steaks with the remaining oil and season with salt and pepper. Cook the steaks for 3 minutes each side for medium or until cooked to your liking. Remove to a plate, cover and rest for 5–10 minutes.

4 Add the mushrooms and marinade to the hot frying pan, tossing often for 5 minutes or until mushrooms are just tender.

5 Thickly slice steaks and arrange on serving plates. Serve with mushrooms and dressed salad, lemon and crispy baked chips.

♥ If you are feeding teenage boys, you may want to add another steak.

# BEEF, BASIL & PEANUT STIR-FRY

*I stir-fry at least once a week because it's quick and healthy and a great way to increase our vegetable intake. We should all be eating 5 serves of fresh vegetables daily.*

SERVES 4

*600g beef fillet, trimmed*
*2 Asian eschalots, peeled, quartered*
*2 large garlic cloves, crushed*
*3cm piece ginger, peeled, sliced*
*1 long red chilli, halved, deseeded, chopped*
*3 tablespoons peanut oil*
*1 small red capsicum cut into thin strips*
*125g green beans, trimmed, cut into 6cm lengths*
*1 tablespoon fish sauce*
*1 tablespoon kecap manis*
*1 bunch Thai basil, leaves removed*
*100g bean sprouts, trimmed* ✿
*¼ cup roasted salted peanuts*
*cooked jasmine rice, to serve*

1 Thinly slice the beef across the grain. (This helps keep the beef tender as it cooks.) Combine the eschalots, garlic, ginger, chilli and 2 teaspoons of the oil in a food processor. Process until very finely chopped. Spoon into a bowl, add the beef and stir to coat.

2 Heat the wok over high heat until hot – don't add the oil as it will burn before the wok is hot enough for cooking. Once hot, add 2 teaspoons oil and swirl to coat the wok. Add one quarter of the beef and stir-fry for 30 seconds until sealed. Remove to a clean bowl. Repeat with oil and beef in three batches. (Cooking meat in batches means the wok stays very hot, searing the meat, not stewing it.)

3 Add the remaining oil and swirl to coat the wok. Add the capsicum and beans and stir-fry for 30 seconds until the vegetables are well coated in the oil. Return all the beef and any juices to the wok with the fish sauce and kecap manis and stir-fry until well coated. Remove from the heat, add the basil, bean sprouts and peanuts, and toss until basil starts to wilt. Serve with rice.

✿ Bean sprouts thrive in cold water. On arriving home from the shops, tip them into a bowl of cold water, cover and refrigerate. Not only will they stay fresh for up to a week, they will remain crisp.

# SPRING SALAD WITH SOFT-BOILED EGG

*I've never stopped learning with my job. I was recently working on an advertising shoot where we needed 12 perfect soft boiled eggs with centred yolks – sounds easy, I know. After 2 hours and many dozen eggs the photographer, Ben Dearnley (also a great mate), suggested the method below. We hit the jackpot! It's fail-proof.*

SERVES 4 AS LIGHT MAIN

*12 thin slices prosciutto*
*100g baby spinach leaves*
*50g snow pea tendrils or baby beetroot leaves*
*1/3 cup mint leaves*
*1 Lebanese cucumber, halved, sliced*
*3 green onions, thinly sliced*
*2 ripe avocadoes, peeled and sliced*
*4 free-range organic eggs, cold from the fridge*

DRESSING

*1/4 cup extra-virgin olive oil*
*1 tablespoon red wine vinegar*
*1/2 small garlic clove, finely chopped*
*1 teaspoon caster sugar*
*1 teaspoon seeded mustard*

1 Heat a large non-stick frying pan over medium-high heat. Cook prosciutto, in batches, for 2–3 minutes each side or until golden. Set aside to cool – that's when it will become crisp.

2 Toss the spinach leaves, snow pea tendrils, mint leaves, cucumber, green onions and avocado in a large bowl, then divide between four plates. Top each plate with 3 pieces proscuitto.

3 Half fill a medium saucepan with water and bring it to the boil over high heat, then stir in 1 teaspoon salt. Pierce a small hole in the larger end of each egg with a sharp safety pin or needle. Lower the cold eggs into the boiling water, leave for 30 seconds, then stir to form a whirlpool in the pan. Boil gently for 5 minutes. Remove the eggs to a large bowl of iced water and stand 3 minutes, then drain and peel.

4 For the dressing, combine all the ingredients in a screw-top jar and shake well to combine.

5 Break the soft-boiled eggs in half and place into the centre of each salad. Spoon over the dressing, season with salt and pepper and serve.

# PAD THAI

*In my first book in this series, **Fast, Fresh & Fabulous**, there were about 8 recipes not photographed, and this is one. Since then, I have had so many emails from people disappointed at not being able to see what it should look like, so forgive me for repeating this recipe – but you now have the pic!*

SERVES 4

*250g pad thai rice stick noodles*
*¼ cup Thai fish sauce*
*2 tablespoons grated palm sugar or brown sugar*
*1 lemon, juiced*
*2 tablespoons cornflour*
*good pinch chilli powder*
*150g firm tofu, diced*
*2½ tablespoons peanut oil*
*2 chicken breast fillets, thinly sliced across the grain*
*3 French eschalots, thinly sliced*
*2 garlic cloves, crushed*
*1 long red chilli, finely chopped*
*1 long green chilli, finely chopped*
*2 eggs, lightly beaten*
*½ cup roasted salted peanuts, chopped*
*125g bean sprouts, trimmed*
*fried shallots, coriander and lemon wedges, to serve* ♥

1 Place the noodles in a large bowl, cover with warm water and set aside for 5 minutes or until the noodles are just tender. ✿ Drain well, then refresh in cold water and drain again. Combine the fish sauce, palm sugar and ¼ cup lemon juice in a jug and stir to dissolve the sugar. Set aside.

2 Place the cornflour and chilli powder into a snap lock bag and shake to combine. Add the tofu and shake gently to coat. Heat wok over medium-high heat until hot. Add 2 teaspoons oil and the tofu and stir-fry gently until the tofu is golden. Remove to a plate and wipe the wok clean.

3 Heat wok over high heat until hot. Add 1 tablespoon of oil and swirl to coat the surface. Add the chicken, stir-fry until golden. Transfer the chicken to a plate. Add 2 teaspoons oil, eschalots, garlic and chillies and stir-fry for 1 minute. Remove to the plate with the chicken.

4 Add the remaining 2 teaspoons oil and the eggs and allow to cook until slightly set. Use a wooden spoon to stir the egg until lightly scrambled. Add the noodles, fish sauce mixture, peanuts, bean sprouts, chicken, spice mixture and tofu. Stir-fry 1–2 minutes or until heated through. Sprinkle with fried shallots and coriander leaves and serve with lemon wedges.

✿ The noodles are critical to the success of the dish. They should still be a little firm at this stage. When they are stir fried in step 4, they soften completly.

♥ Once you have opened fried shallots, store them in the freezer so they don't turn rancid.

# HANOI CRISPY SPRING ROLLS

*Hanoi is the most beautiful place I have ever travelled to – beautiful land, beautiful people and beautiful food. These reheat really well, so don't be put off by the cooking process.*

MAKES 12

*50g dried rice vermicelli noodles*
*350g pork mince*
*170g can crab meat, well drained*
*3 garlic cloves, crushed*
*¼ cup coriander leaves, finely chopped*
*3 green onions, thinly sliced*
*1 tablespoon fish sauce*
*2 cups warm water*
*1 tablespoon caster sugar*
*12 round (22cm) rice paper wrappers*
*vegetable or peanut oil, for deep-frying*
*12 iceberg lettuce leaves, trimmed to serve*
*1 cup mint leaves*
*1 cup coriander leaves*
*Lebanese cucumber strips, to serve*

CHILLI DIPPING SAUCE

*2 garlic cloves, chopped*
*1 red banana chilli, deseeded, roughly chopped*
*1 red Birdseye chilli, seeds in, roughly chopped*
*2 tablespoons grated palm sugar or brown sugar*
*1 large lime, juiced*
*¼ cup fish sauce*
*½ cup cold tap water*

1 For the chilli dipping sauce, combine garlic and chillies in a food processor. Process until finely chopped, then transfer to a clean jar. Add the remaining ingredients and refrigerate for 2 hours or overnight if time allows, shaking occasionally to dissolve the sugar.

2 Place the noodles in a heat-proof bowl. Cover with hot water. Stand for 10 minutes or until just tender. Drain well, then roughly chop and place into a large bowl. Add the pork, crab, garlic, coriander, green onions and fish sauce. Mix well using clean hands.

3 Line a tray with a damp tea towel. Combine the warm water and caster sugar in a large round shallow dish. Dip 1 rice paper wrapper in water mixture for 5 seconds. ✿ Place on a tea towel and allow to stand 30–50 seconds until it softens enough to roll. Top with 2 tablespoons of the filling along one edge, then roll the wrapper over the filling, folding in the sides and rolling up tightly to enclose the filling. Repeat using remaining rice paper wrappers and filling.

4 Preheat the oven to 230°C fan-forced/230°C no fan. Heat the oil in a wok or deep-fryer over medium heat until hot. Place a wire rack over a baking tray. Cook the spring rolls, in batches, for 5 minutes or until golden. Use a slotted spoon to remove to the wire rack. Once they are all cooked, place into hot oven on the rack for 5–8 minutes to warm through and crisp up.

5 Place spring roll on top of lettuce leaves. Top with mint, coriander and cucumber. Serve with chilli dipping sauce.

✿ The trick to using rice paper roll pastry is not to dip them in water too long – after 5 seconds remove from the water. It will still be firm, but allowing it to stand softens the sheet enough for easy rolling. Once you try it, hopefully you make them more often.

# WOK-FRIED BURMESE-STYLE SNAKE BEANS

*I just love this dish. You can replace the snake beans with green beans, asparagus or gai lan. Slap a Post-it note on this page – I promise you'll love it too once you make it.*

SERVES 4 AS SIDE

*3 garlic cloves, peeled*
*1 long red chilli, deseeded, roughly chopped*
*1 long green chilli, deseeded, roughly chopped*
*½ cup roasted salted peanuts*
*2 teaspoons grated jaggery or palm sugar* ✿
*2 teaspoons peanut oil*
*1 bunch snake beans, trimmed, cut into 6cm lengths, washed*
*¼ cup coconut milk*

1 Using a mortar and pestle or small food processor, pound or process the garlic, chillies, peanuts and sugar to a paste.

2 Heat a wok over medium-high heat until hot. Add the oil and swirl to coat the wok. Add the chilli-and-peanut paste and cook, stirring constantly, for 1 minute or until aromatic. Add the snake beans and a splash of water and stir-fry 1–2 minutes until the beans are almost tender.

3 Add the coconut milk and stir until just coated. Pile onto a serving plate and serve with beef, chicken or fish.

✿ Jaggery is an unrefined yellowy-brown coloured sugar made from boiled sugar cane juice. It's sold in large lumps in Indian and Thai stores and should be sticky and easy to crumble, grate or chop. Palm sugar is a suitable substitute.

You can slightly undercook the beans and remove from heat and allow to cool. Stir through shredded chicken, duck or prawns and serve as a main meal salad.

# ASPARAGUS WITH BALSAMIC FIG GLAZE

*The sweet, sticky glaze coating the crisp, tender asparagus is the perfect way to get the family to eat more vegetables. It's absolutely delicious and great served with chicken, pork or sausages.*

SERVES 4 AS SIDE

*1 tablespoon flaked almonds*
*20g butter*
*2 tablespoons fig paste* ✿
*1 tablespoon balsamic vinegar*
*2 bunches asparagus, ends trimmed, washed*
*1 tablespoon currants*

1 Scatter the almonds over the base of a medium non-stick frying pan and place over medium-high heat. Cook 4–5 minutes, tossing the almonds often until light golden and toasted. Remove the almonds to a plate.

2 Add the butter, fig paste and balsamic vinegar to the hot pan and stir until melted and smooth. Add the asparagus, currants and 1–2 tablespoons of warm water if necessary, ♥ cover with a lid or piece of baking paper and cook 3–4 minutes, shaking the pan often, until the asparagus is just tender and well coated in the glaze.

3 Transfer the glazed asparagus to a serving plate, scatter over the almonds, season with salt and pepper, and serve.

✿ Maggie Beer brand fig paste is available at most deli supermarkets. Alternatively, fig jam or ginger marmalade is delicious.

♥ The water is not always necessary – it will depend on the thickness of the asparagus spears and their freshness. Only add if the glaze becomes very thick.

# SPRING SWEET

# LEMON MERINGUE GELATO

*You may look at this recipe and think, 'Too hard – it's easy to buy.' Believe me, like everything home-made, this is sooo much better and well worth the effort.*

SERVES 8

*6 large lemons, juiced*
*1¼ cup caster sugar*
*6 free-range egg yolks*
*2 cups full-cream milk, warmed* ♥
*80g meringues, crushed*

♥ To warm the milk, pour into a 3- or 4-cup capacity heat-proof jug and microwave, uncovered, for 3 minutes on High/100%. Stir well to distribute the heat before using.

1 Combine 1¼ cups freshly squeezed lemon juice and ½ cup of the caster sugar in a medium saucepan. Place over medium heat and bring to a simmer, stirring until the sugar dissolves. Pour into a jug and refrigerate until cold. Wash and dry the saucepan.

2 Using an electric hand mixer, beat the egg yolks and remaining ¾ cup caster sugar together until thick and pale. Add the warm milk, whisking on low until combined. Pour the mixture into the saucepan. Stir over a medium heat for 8 minutes or until the custard thickens and coats the back of a metal spoon (do not boil). Pour into a bowl, cover the surface with plastic wrap and refrigerate until cold.

3 Slowly pour the cold lemon syrup into the cold custard, whisking constantly, then pour into a 4-cup capacity airtight container. Cover and freeze 8–12 hours or until set.

4 Spoon the mixture into a food processor and process until smooth. Return to the airtight container and swirl through the crushed meringues. Cover the surface with plastic wrap then a lid and freeze overnight or until set.

Check the consistency before serving – you may need to transfer the container from the freezer to the fridge for 15 minutes to soften the gelato slightly before serving. As there are no preservatives, home-made gelato sets more firmly than purchased ones.

# LITTLE CHOCOLATE MACAROON TARTS

*I have been trying to master this macaroon pastry for years after tasting something similar at a little cake shop in the Southern Highlands of New South Wales. Finally, success – these tarts taste even better than they look.*

MAKES 24

*300g quality dark chocolate, chopped, (Plaistowe brand)*
*300ml thickened cream*
*2 tablespoons caster sugar*
*2 eggs, lightly beaten*
*2 tablespoons strong brewed espresso or coffee liqueur (like Kahlúa)*
*200g fresh raspberries and cocoa powder, to serve*

MACAROON PASTRY

*2½ cups desiccated coconut*
*⅔ cup caster sugar*
*½ cup plain flour*
*3 eggs, lightly beaten*

1 Preheat the oven and a large flat tray to 200°C fan-forced/200°C no fan. Lightly grease a twelve-hole, 2-tablespoon (40ml) capacity, flat-based patty tray. Line the base of each hole with a round of baking paper. ✿

2 For the macaroon pastry, combine coconut, sugar and flour in a bowl. Add the eggs and mix until well combined and a little sticky. Using one firmly packed tablespoon of mixture per tart, use your fingertips to press the mixture into the base and side of each hole, dipping your fingertips in cold water to prevent it from sticking to your fingers.

3 Place the patty tray onto the hot tray in the oven and bake for 7 minutes or until light golden around the edges. ♥ Remove from the oven and reduce the temperature to 180°C fan-forced/190°C no fan.

4 Combine the chocolate and cream in a heat-proof, microwave-safe bowl. Microwave uncovered for 2 minutes on High/100%, stirring every minute with a metal spoon until smooth. Stir in the sugar and eggs, then the coffee. Pour the chocolate mixture into the warm coconut shells. Return to the oven and bake for 10 minutes or until the filling is set.

5 Allow the tarts to cool for 10 minutes in the pan, then carefully loosen the edge of each tart with a table knife and remove to a wire rack. Repeat with remaining coconut pastry and filling to make another 12 tarts.

6 Top the tarts with raspberries, dust with cocoa and serve warm or at room temperature.

✿ Lining the base of each hole is your insurance policy that they are easy to remove once baked.

♥ If the pastry puffs up during baking, use a small teaspoon to press it back into shape while it's hot.

# JANELLE'S LEMONADE SCONES

*In 2010 I took part in a 'scone off' on Channel 7's* Sunrise. *I was inundated with over 800 requests for the recipe in the days that followed. So, for those of you who missed it, here it is with my famous lemon curd.*

MAKES 20

*4 cups self-raising flour*
*300ml pouring cream*
*300–350ml chilled lemonade*
*double cream, to serve*

MICROWAVE LEMON CURD

*3 free-range eggs*
*2 free-range egg yolks*
*¾ cup caster sugar*
*1 lemon, rind finely grated*
*4 large lemons, juiced*
*125g butter, chilled, cubed*

♥ Each time the scone mixture is rolled out, the scones cut from the mixture won't rise as high as the previous scones, so rolling a little thicker compensates for this – fingers crossed all your scones will now be the same!

1 For the microwave lemon curd, combine eggs, egg yolks, sugar and lemon rind in a 6-cup capacity, heat-proof, microwave-safe bowl. Beat with a balloon whisk until combined, then add ¾ cup lemon juice, whisking constantly. Add the butter. Microwave, uncovered, for 7–10 minutes on Medium/50%, whisking every minute until the mixture just comes to the boil. Pour into sterilised jars, seal and label. Refrigerate until ready to use.

2 Preheat the oven to 230°C fan-forced/250°C no fan. Lightly grease a large flat oven tray.

3 Sift the flour into a large bowl. Add the pouring cream and 300ml lemonade. Use a table knife to stir to a soft dough, adding more lemonade if necessary. Turn onto a lightly floured surface and knead gently until the dough comes together.

4 Press or roll the dough out to a 2cm-thick round disk. Use a 5½ cm round cutter dipped in flour and cut as many scones from the dough as possible. Gently press the unused dough together then press or roll the dough to 2½cm thick this time. ♥ Cut more scones. Repeat with the unused dough, making it a little thicker each time before cutting the scones.

5 Place scones onto the tray almost touching each other. Bake for 12–15 minutes until golden and well risen. Serve hot with lemon curd or jam and cream.

# CHOCOLATE CHERRY COCONUT SLICE

*During my time as a magazine food editor, I wrote a version of this recipe for a cover – it was one of our best-selling issues of all time. Chocolate, cherry and coconut is loved by almost everyone, me included.*

MAKES 24

*1 cup plain flour*
*½ cup brown sugar*
*3½ cups desiccated coconut*
*125g butter, melted*
*395g can Nestlé sweetened condensed milk*
*2 eggs, lightly beaten*
*200g red glacé cherries, chopped*

CHOCOLATE TOP

*200g quality dark chocolate (Plaistowe brand)*
*¼ cup pouring cream*

1 Preheat the oven to 170°C fan-forced/180°C no fan. Line the base and sides of a 3cm-deep, 18.5cm x 28cm (base) slab pan, allowing a 2cm overhang of baking paper at both long ends.

2 Combine the flour, brown sugar and ½ cup of the coconut in a bowl. Add the warm butter and stir to combine. Press the mixture over the base of the prepared pan. Bake for 10–15 minutes or until light golden.

3 Combine the condensed milk, eggs and remaining coconut in a bowl, then fold in the cherries. Spoon the cherry filling over the warm base, then return to the oven to bake for 18–20 minutes or until set in the centre. Set aside to cool completely.

4 For the chocolate top, combine the chocolate and cream in a heat-proof, microwave-safe bowl. Microwave uncovered in 1-minute bursts on High/100%, stirring every minute with a metal spoon until smooth.

5 Spread the warm chocolate over the room-temperature cherry filling. Set aside until firm. Cut into pieces using a warm knife.

# JIMMI JUMBLES

*My sisters and I used to love it when we would find a packet of these in the cupboard, though I think they were supposed to be for Dad. As always, home-made jumbles are so much better.*

MAKES 36

*60g butter, chopped*
*¼ cup firmly packed brown sugar*
*¼ cup golden syrup*
*¼ cup honey*
*2 teaspoons ground cinnamon*
*2 teaspoons ground ginger*
*1½ cups plain flour*
*½ teaspoon bicarbonate of soda*

ICING

*3 cups icing sugar*
*½ lemon, juiced*
*1–2 tablespoons boiling water*
*pink food colouring, optional*
*hundreds and thousands, to decorate, optional*

1 Preheat oven to 160°C fan-forced/170°C no fan. Line 3 baking trays with baking paper. Combine the butter, sugar, golden syrup and honey in a small saucepan. Stir over medium heat until the butter melts, then bring to the boil. Remove from the heat and quickly transfer to a mixing bowl. Stir the cinnamon and ginger into the hot mixture, then set aside for 5 minutes.

2 Sift the flour and bicarbonate of soda together over the spice mixture. Stir until well combined. Roll heaped teaspoonfuls of dough into balls and place onto the trays. Flatten the balls slightly with your fingertips.

3 Bake for 8–10 minutes or until the edges are firm to touch. Allow to cool for 15 minutes on trays before removing to a wire rack to cool.

4 For the icing, sift the icing sugar into a microwave-safe, heat-proof bowl. Add 2 tablespoons lemon juice and stir to form a very thick paste, adding boiling water if required. Remove half the icing to another bowl and add a few drops of pink food colouring to it. Mix well.

5 Microwave the white icing, uncovered, for 30–40 seconds on High/100% or until warm and runny. Using half the jumbles, dip the top into the warm icing, then sprinkle with hundreds and thousands straightaway. ♥ Turn upright to set. Repeat with pink icing and remaining jumbles.

♥ Once the biscuits hit the icing it sets quite quickly, so as you turn the biscuit upright sprinkle with hundreds and thousands.

# WATERMELON SORBET WITH VANILLA SUGAR BERRIES

*My mum spent quite some time in hospital this year, so I was dropping care packages in to Dad every night after our shoot – this is one of his favourite desserts in this book.*

SERVES 8

*2 cups white sugar*
*1 cup cold tap water*
*5kg (1 small) seedless watermelon, peeled, chopped*
*2 egg whites*

VANILLA SUGAR BERRIES

*750g mixed fresh berries*
*2 tablespoons vanilla sugar (see recipe page 178)*
*1 teaspoon pomegranate molasses (see recipe page 212)*

✿ While this process seems fiddly, it's important since it breaks down the ice crystals so that the sorbet is smooth and silky, not icy.

1 Combine the white sugar and water into a medium saucepan over medium-high heat. Cook, stirring, for 5 minutes or until syrup comes to the boil. Remove from the heat and set aside to cool for 30 minutes.

2 Meanwhile, blend the watermelon in batches until smooth. Strain the watermelon puree through a sieve into a jug, pressing with the back of a spoon to extract as much liquid as possible. (You should have about 1.5 litres/6 cups of watermelon juice.) Stir the sugar syrup into the watermelon juice, then pour into a shallow 8-cup capacity airtight container. Cover and freeze for 6–12 hours until almost set.

3 Break up the sorbet with a metal spoon, then transfer to a food processor. Pulse until the sorbet is smooth with a soft, icy texture. Return the sorbet to the container and freeze overnight or until firm . ✿

4 Using an electric hand mixer, beat the egg white to soft peaks. Spoon the watermelon mixture into a food processor again and process until smooth (not melted). Transfer to a large bowl and fold through egg whites. Spoon the sorbet back into the airtight container, cover the surface with plastic wrap then a lid and freeze overnight.

5 For the vanilla sugar berries, place berries in a large ceramic dish. Sprinkle over the sugar, then drizzle over the pomegranate molasses. Toss gently to coat all the berries. Cover and refrigerate for 1 hour.

6 Spoon the berries and some of the juices that have formed onto serving plates and serve with scoops of watermelon sorbet.

# LITTLE PASSIONFRUIT SPONGE CAKES

*Sponge and pavlova always haunted me throughout my years of training, but since then I have realised it's about having a great recipe and a positive attitude.*

MAKES 12

*½ cup cornflour*
*½ teaspoon cream of tartar*
*¼ teaspoon bicarbonate of soda*
*2 x 59g free-range eggs, at room temperature*
*⅓ cup caster sugar*
*1 tablespoon pure icing sugar*
*300ml thickened cream, whipped*

PASSIONFRUIT ICING

*2 cups icing sugar*
*1 passionfruit, halved*
*hot water*

♥ For one large sponge, double the recipe above and bake in two 20cm (base) sandwich pans for 15 minutes at the same temperature in step 1.

1 Preheat the oven to 160°C fan-forced/ 180°C no fan. Grease twelve, ½-cup capacity muffin holes, then line the base of each hole with a round of baking paper. Sift the cornflour, cream of tartar and bicarbonate of soda together twice.

2 Using an electric mixer, beat the eggs, caster sugar and icing sugar together on high speed for 3–5 minutes or until thick, pale and creamy. Sift the flour mixture again over the egg mixture, then use a large metal spoon to gently fold the flour in until combined.

3 Half fill each muffin hole with the sponge mixture. Bake for 13–15 minutes or until a skewer inserted into the centre comes out clean and the sponge shrinks a little from the edge. Allow to stand in the tray for 3 minutes before loosening the edge of each sponge cake and turning onto a wire rack covered with a sheet of baking paper. Remove the baking paper rounds from the base of each sponge and set aside to cool.

4 Trim the tops of the sponge cakes if necessary so that when turned upside down they will sit flat. Cut each cake in half using a serrated knife. Place trimmed side down onto a serving plate lined with baking paper. Fill the centre of each sponge with cream, sandwiching them back together.

5 For the passionfruit icing, sift the icing sugar into a heat-proof bowl and add passionfruit pulp and enough hot water to form a thick paste. Place bowl over a saucepan of simmering water and stir until the icing is warm and runny. Spoon the warm icing over the sponge cakes and serve.

# CHOCOLATE HAZELNUT SPREAD

*Why would you make your own chocolate hazelnut spread? Well, why not? You know exactly what's in it.*

MAKES 1¼ CUPS

*⅓ cup (50g) hazelnuts, roasted ♥*
*½ cup skim-milk powder*
*⅓ cup caster sugar*
*3 tablespoons cocoa powder*
*1 tablespoon cornflour*
*200ml full-cream milk*
*1 tablespoon olive oil*

1 Place the hazelnuts in a small food processor and process until finely ground.

2 Combine the milk powder, caster sugar, cocoa powder and cornflour in a medium saucepan. Gradually whisk in the cold milk. Add the hazelnuts and oil. Cook, stirring constantly, over medium-high heat for 5 minutes or until the spread comes together as a thick paste. (Keep stirring to prevent it sticking to the base.)

3 Spoon the hot chocolate spread into a hot sterilised jar and set aside, uncovered, to cool. Cover, then refrigerate.

♥ To roast hazelnuts, spread them over a baking tray and place in a preheated 180°C fan-forced/200°C no fan oven for 8 minutes or until the skins crack. Transfer the hazelnuts to a clean tea towel and rub firmly to remove the skins.

The spread will keep in the fridge for at least 3 weeks.

# MUM'S OVALTINE BUN

*This is my Mum's all-time most-requested recipe. It would turn up in our lunch boxes, on a plate after school and piled high at every pool party we ever had growing up, which was almost every weekend. When I close my eyes and remember this, I see a half dozen families having the time of their lives. My mum would want you to share this with your family and friends to create your own happy memories.*

SERVES 8

*1½ cups full-cream milk*
*1 tablespoon golden syrup*
*2 cups self-raising flour*
*1 teaspoon bicarbonate of soda*
*½ cup caster sugar*
*6 tablespoons Ovaltine powder*
*1 cup sultanas*
*butter and golden syrup, to serve*

1 Preheat the oven to 160°C fan-forced/180°C no fan. Grease and line base and sides of a 7cm-deep, 10.5cm x 21cm (base) loaf pan.

2 Combine the milk and golden syrup in a small saucepan over medium heat for 3–5 minutes until the syrup has dissolved and the milk is lukewarm.

3 Sift the flour and bicarbonate of soda into a bowl. Add the sugar, Ovaltine and sultanas, then stir to combine. Pour the warm milk over the Ovaltine mixture and stir until well combined. Stand in the bowl for 5 minutes, ♥ then pour the mixture into the prepared pan.

4 Bake for 50–60 minutes or until a skewer inserted into the centre comes out clean. Stand in the pan for 10 minutes, then turn onto a wire rack. Slice and serve warm with butter and golden syrup. It's awesome toasted as well.

♥ Allowing the mixture to stand before it goes into the pan means it thickens slightly so that the sultanas won't all fall to the bottom of the pan while cooking.

# ACKNOWLEDGEMENTS

*'Thank you' is a phrase that's overused, and maybe under-appreciated, but in this case it come from my heart to all those people whose names appear below.*

I am indebted to my amazing family, who continue to support and inspire me to achieve my professional dreams. My family means everything to me and I love them dearly.

To the special people whom I call my friends – you know I don't use that word lightly. With this book completed, I look forward to spending more quality time over coffee or bubbles and home-made cake in the year that follows.

My publisher, Random House Australia, with special mention to Nikki Christer, the publishing director who acted as my publisher on this book (how cool is it to have a company director so hands-on?), and Anna Govender, who managed every process of this book with a level of care every author dreams of. My editor, Brandon VanOver, whose gentle nature and phenomenal eye gives me great confidence. Jo Penney in production, thank you for your attention to detail. The editorial, sales and marketing teams who support and maintain the presence of my books in stores; Shannon Lane, my publicist; and Jay Ryves and her design team.

Steve Brown, one of this country's best food photographers and a dear friend, who has shot all four of my books with each one getting better and better. Thank you for labouring over every shot and casting your expert eye over how they fall on the page – thank you just doesn't seem enough.

Kate Nichols, one of the beautiful people I feel honoured to call a friend and colleague. Thanks for cooking every recipe for photography – a huge ask, I know, questioning each little detail, leaving nothing to chance for my readers and, most of all, picking up your phone every time you see JB on the caller ID – love you.

Alex and Carla, my makeover team – it gets harder each year, I know, but hugs and kisses to you both for the great wardrobe, hair and make-up on the cover and images of me throughout this book. Thanks, Carl, for allowing us to invade your space for a day's shoot. To Shelley at Mud Ceramics for giving me access to borrow beautiful things with no strings attached.

Thanks to Sue Dodd, whom I consider one of this country's leading fresh produce gurus, for helping me finetune my best buys information and continually sharing your knowledge and passion for fresh seasonal produce. And to all the greengrocers, butchers, dairy merchants, stall holders at farmers' markets, who constantly keep me supplied with updated information – it's knowledge I value and have now been able to share with my readers.

Special mention to the families at Ronald McDonald House Randwick – your courage and stories put life, family, friends and work into perspective and inspire me to be grateful for today.

Janelle xoxo

# INDEX

## T



## V



## W



## Y

AVAILABLE NOW AT
ALL GOOD BOOKSTORES

*www.janellebloom.com.au*

An Ebury Press book
Published by Random House Australia Pty Ltd
Level 3, 100 Pacific Highway, North Sydney NSW 2060
www.randomhouse.com.au

First published by Ebury Press 2011

Text copyright © Janelle Bloom 2011
Photographs copyright © Steve Brown 2011

The moral right of the author has been asserted.

All rights reserved. No part of this book may be reproduced or transmitted by any person or entity, including internet search engines or retailers, in any form or by any means, electronic or mechanical, including photocopying (except under the statutory exceptions provisions of the Australian *Copyright Act 1968*), recording, scanning or by any information storage and retrieval system without the prior written permission of Random House Australia.

Addresses for companies within Random House Group can be found at
www.randomhouse.com.au/offices

National Library of Australia
Cataloguing-in-Publication Entry

Bloom, Janelle.
My Favourite Food for All Seasons / Janelle Bloom.
ISBN 978 1 74275 113 9 (pbk.)
Seasonal Cooking.
Cooking
Food supply – Seasonal variations.

641.564

Photography by Steve Brown
Cover and internal design by Jay Ryves and Naomi Solomon at Future Classic
Printed and bound by Imago in China

10 9 8 7 6 5 4 3 2 1